Old Europe, New Europe, Core Europe

Transatlantic Relations After the Iraq War

◆

DANIEL LEVY, MAX PENSKY, and JOHN TORPEY

VERSO

London • New York

First published by Verso 2005
© in the collection, Verso 2005
© in the contributions, the individual contributors/
original publications

3 5 7 9 10 8 6 4 2

Verso
UK: 6 Meard Street, London W1F 0EG
USA: 180 Varick Street, New York, NY 10014–4606
www.versobooks.com

Verso is the imprint of New Left Books

ISBN 1–84467–520–3 (Paperback)
ISBN 1–84467–018–X (Hardback)

British Library Cataloguing in Publication Data
Old Europe, new Europe, core Europe
1. Habermas, Jurgen – Views on European cooperation
2. European cooperation 3. Europe – Foreign relations –
United States 4. United States – Foreign relations – Europe
5. Europe – Foreign relations – 1989– 6. United States –
Foreign relations – 2001–
I. Levy, Daniel II. Pensky, Max, 1961– III. Torpey, John C.
327.4'073

Library of Congress Cataloging-in-Publication Data
A catalog record for this book is available from the Library of Congress

Typeset in Garamond
Printed in the USA by Courier Companies, Inc

CONTENTS

3 FURTHER REFLECTIONS

ACKNOWLEDGMENTS

The editors would like to thank the contributors for their assistance in bringing this effort to completion. We owe a debt of gratitude to the translators at the Center for Research in Translation (CRIT) at Binghamton University for their efforts in translating the texts included here that were not originally written in English.

We would also like to thank Sima Godfrey and David Page of the Institute for European Studies at the University of British Columbia for their assistance with this project. Their help brought to fruition an endeavor that, without their support, would have taken much longer to complete.

EDITORS' INTRODUCTION

Daniel Levy, Max Pensky, and John Torpey

On May 31, 2003, articles on the state of European–American relations by several of Europe's leading intellectual figures (along with one American) appeared in leading dailies in Germany, France, Italy, Spain, and Switzerland. This unprecedented intervention in European public discussion was organized and coordinated by Germany's leading philosopher and public intellectual, Jürgen Habermas, in an effort to stimulate discussion of Europe's place in the (transatlantic) world in the aftermath of the Iraq war. Habermas himself wrote an essay in the *Frankfurter Allgemeine Zeitung* that was published under his name and that of the French philosopher Jacques Derrida. It was an unusual alliance; the two have more often argued over philosophical matters than agreed about them, but here they decided that the political exigencies overrode any previous differences. Pleading difficult personal circumstances, Derrida appended a short preface but did not write his own piece; instead, the Habermas-penned essay appeared in French translation in *Libération*. The Habermas–Derrida manifesto invoked the notion of a 'core Europe' – distinct from both the British and the 'new' European candidates for EU membership and defined above all by its secular, Enlightenment, and social-democratic traditions – and sought to build a common European identity upon those traditions.

The other contributions came from renowned Italian writer Umberto Eco in *La Repubblica* and philosopher Gianni Vattimo in *La Stampa*; from Swiss writer and newly installed President of the Academy of Arts in Berlin, Adolf Muschg, in the *Neue Zürcher Zeitung*, Spanish philosopher Fernando Savater in *El País*, and – riding shotgun, so to speak – the American philosopher Richard Rorty in the *Süddeutsche Zeitung*. This concerted effort triggered immediate responses among an array of prominent intellectuals on either side of the Atlantic. As a result of this intervention, the *feuilleton* ('Arts & Ideas') sections of the German-speaking press became the arena for a wide-ranging and illuminating debate about the nature of the transatlantic Alliance, revealing diverging conceptions of how the European project should unfold and exploring Europe's future relationships both with the US and with itself in the face of the eastward expansion of the European Union.

Renowned as a philosopher of the 'public sphere' – the space between organized government and market economy where citizens can raise and argue over issues of mutual interest in a free and open manner – Habermas has also been Germany's most visible and influential public intellectual for decades. While frequently contributing to debates in German (and other national) print media, this time Habermas went further than ever before in putting into practice his theory of the role of national media within political public spheres. By inviting prominent and visible authors and academics to participate, and by arranging for the appearance of their articles across a European public sphere to coincide with that of his own, Habermas succeeded in organizing a debate over a crucial moment in Europe's political life in a virtually unprecedented manner.

This volume aims to make available to an English-speaking audience some of the important new debates that have emerged in Europe from the divisions between 'old Europe' and the Anglo-American–'new' European alliance over the decision to invade Iraq. This 'documentation' of the discussion is intended to provide readers in the Anglophone world with access to the debate, and the opportunity to follow for themselves the discussions taking place among leading European intellectuals and their American interlocutors regarding the future of European–American relations and that of unifying Europe itself.

Naturally, the contributors to the volume have different perspectives that may be a matter of varied experiences shaped by geographical, generational, and political circumstances. As editors we had to make a decision as to whether we would divide the individual pieces thematically or stick to a chronological approach. We opted for the latter, supplementing this mundane procedure by offering a more thematic treatment in this introduction. To further enrich the volume we have also included a number of essays that were not directly part of the debate that played out in the pages of the German press, but that nonetheless address many of the issues that arose in connection with the Habermas–Derrida initiative. Thus the first section of the book contains the original contributions by Habermas and the others whom he invited to publish their pieces as part of the initiative; the second section contains the responses to the initiative; and the last section collects a number of articles that appeared elsewhere, or were specially commissioned for this volume.

Europe in the Mirror of Transatlantic Relations

The first round of essays, by Habermas, Derrida, Eco, Savater, Vattimo, and Rorty, sought to analyze the situation in which Europeans found themselves – especially vis-à-vis their long-time Cold War ally, the United States – after the one-sided decision-making about the Iraq war in which the latter had engaged, along with Britain, on the road to the invasion. Almost as one, the publics of West European countries – 'in London and Rome, Madrid and Barcelona, Berlin and Paris,' as Habermas put it – had taken to the streets on February 15 in the largest numbers since the Second World War to demonstrate their opposition to the ever-advancing drumbeat of war. The scene played out against the background of a surreptitiously organized 'Letter of Eight,' signed by the heads of state of eight countries (Spain, Poland, Hungary, Czech Republic, Italy, Denmark, Portugal, and the United Kingdom), supporting the US-led effort to search out and eliminate Saddam Hussein's putative weapons of mass destruction – or, alternatively, to liberate the Iraqi people from the iron grip of Saddam's brutal regime and to democratize the Middle East, depending on the war's justification *du jour*. Habermas thought he glimpsed in the demonstrations of February 15 'a sign for the birth of a European public sphere.' Against the background of serious transatlantic differences over the legitimacy of the war, Habermas argued that it was necessary finally to create a Europe that can 'counterbalance the hegemonic unilateralism of the United States.'

Given the halting progress of European unification thus far, Habermas asserted that this project entailed that a 'core Europe' – essentially the Franco-German duo, together with the Benelux countries and Italy – would have to act as a 'locomotive' pulling the train of a common foreign and security policy. Despite the invocation of an 'avant-gardist' notion of the role of 'core Europe,' Habermas insisted that the idea ought not to be misunderstood as a 'Small Europe' that excludes others. Yet the urgency of the need to develop a counterweight to American power trumped any concerns about a 'two-speed' unification process.

Still, a 'Europe' that would be effective on the international stage would require an entity to which ordinary Europeans felt more emotionally attached than they have so far. Heretofore, 'Europe' has amounted to little more than a common currency and an anomalous, undefinable political structure – neither yet a state nor a confederation of states – embodied chiefly in a remote bureaucracy in Brussels. It has certainly not been a 'nation' in any affective sense, commanding the loyalty of significant numbers of people to the point that they are prepared to die on its behalf. Hence the project of a common foreign and security policy raises the challenge of promoting a sense of common belonging among Europeans – the question of a European 'identity.' The issue cannot be avoided; many have doubted that it was possible to create such a supranational identity, and that the European project would ultimately prove stillborn.

In his many writings on the transformations of German politics and society in the process of unification, Habermas has frequently invoked an idea of 'constitutional patriotism' as the only ethically acceptable foundation for national identification.[1] The universal principles of the democratic constitutional state – equal freedom under the law, the ideals of public and private self-determination, and social solidarity based on mutual belonging in a constitutional project – are the only acceptable bases for a national identity that has definitively moved beyond the various *völkisch* claims of ethnic, racial, linguistic, or cultural particularity. Constitutions are historical projects of political communities, and national political cultures can and indeed must engage in ongoing debates on the best, fullest realization of the universal political ideals that their constitution embodies. National history, in turn, can be a source of national pride and cohesion as it embodies the narrative of collective struggle for the realization of the principles of the democratic constitutional state under the specific historical conditions of a national polity.

Does this ideal of constitutional patriotism – which has been widely criticized as too abstract and 'cold' to serve as an adequate foundation for national unity[2] – become more convincing if it is transferred from the national-state level to that of a rapidly integrating European Union? It is this central question on the future of Europe that leads Habermas to claim that Europeans are bound together in a common political and social project, and can collectively appeal to a number of specifically European characteristics.

These binding characteristics were, according to Habermas, secularism in politics; broad popular agreement on calming the maelstrom of capitalism's 'creative destruction'; an appreciation of the paradoxes and pitfalls of technological progress; an ethic of solidarity over the prerogatives of individualism; familiarity with the potential brutality of state power (and hence the abandonment of the death penalty); recognition of limits to the rights of state sovereignty; and a more self-critical attitude with regard to weaker outsiders that flowed from the experience of decolonization. In these features, 'Europeanness' was contrasted rather sharply with the characteristics of American society, which was portrayed as less secular, more violent and bellicose, and as cultivating a more unforgiving variant of capitalism. Thus, for example, Habermas wrote that, 'for us, a president who opens his daily business with public prayer, and associates his significant political decisions with a divine mission, is hard to imagine.' Habermas seemed almost to be trying to 'out-Tocqueville Tocqueville' in his portrayal of the distinctiveness of American society vis-à-vis Europe. The invidiousness of the comparison was surprising in view of Habermas's long-standing efforts to appropriate American styles of philosophy and political thought in the project of re-orienting post-Holocaust German society unambiguously toward 'the West.'

What one might characterize as Habermas's 'reverse Tocquevillean' analysis of transatlantic relations was striking. In fact, Habermas's intervention strongly echoed an article by Dominique Strauss-Kahn from March 2003, in which Strauss-Kahn had claimed, 'On Saturday, February 15, 2003, a nation was born on the streets. This nation is the European nation.'[3] The tone of Habermas' essay was such that one might even be tempted to say that it was tantamount to a European Declaration of Independence, announcing – with 'a decent respect to the opinions of mankind' – why it has become necessary 'to dissolve the political bands' that have connected Europe to the United States since 1945.[4]

The other pieces recruited by Habermas varied in outlook. Gianni Vattimo invoked the notion that, in the end, what makes his readers Europeans and not Americans is that they have 'a different view of existence, a different notion of what

constitutes a "good life," a different existential plan.' Adolf
Muschg spoke of the enormous historical achievement reflected
in the fact that it had become inconceivable for the French and
the Germans – whose antagonisms had fuelled at least a century
of European warfare – to go to war against each other. Muschg
went on to suggest that 'what holds Europe together and what
divides it, are at heart the same thing: common memories and
habits, acquired step by step through the process of distancing
oneself from fatal habits.' Fernando Savater also stressed the
lessons from the past. For him, 'the two tragic world wars that
broke out in our continent have convinced most Europeans
that it is essential to search for internationally regulated formulas
to prevent, avoid, and solve, as a last resort, confrontations
between opposing interests, on a scale beyond nation-state
boundaries.' As a consequence, Savater assigned Europe a
'civilizing' role in a world of interdependencies. In his essay,
Richard Rorty implored Europeans to talk sense into the
American public and to secure 'back-up' for those Americans
who were critical of the Iraq adventure and forced into a
marginal role by the propaganda steamroller created by George
Bush in the aftermath of '9/11.'

In contrast to the other pieces, however, Umberto Eco
focused little on any antagonism between Europe and the
United States, invoking instead a common 'occidental civilization … without this kind of civilization distinguishing Europe
specifically.' Rather than a relationship between the United
States and Europe in which the values of each increasingly
diverged, Eco suggested that, with the United States increasingly oriented to Asia, Europe is likely to decline in comparative
significance. If it wishes to occupy the position of a 'third pole'
between Asia and the United States, he argued, Europe must
'become European' by developing an effective common defense
and foreign policy. 'Otherwise it will become, no offense to
anyone, Guatemala.'

European C(h)ores: Regional Responses

The initiative, but above all Habermas's article itself, provoked an immediate and intense critical response among commentators in the German-speaking press. Interventions came from all corners of Europe. These replies not only spanned a wide geographic range, they also touched on a broad spectrum of themes that are ultimately as much about fault lines within Europe and its search for a common identity as they are about the state of transatlantic relations. What should we make of this controversy, which points to serious disagreement both across the Atlantic and within Europe itself? Is this a consequential matter? How deeply rooted is the transatlantic rift? What brought it on (even Habermas says that 'the Iraq crisis was only a catalyst')? What difference does it make whether Europe and the United States remain close allies? What does the dispute say about the progress of 'Europe'? In what follows, we examine these questions from several points of view.

The Military–Political Dimension

There is a pervasive critique of recent unilateral moves by the United States and its unabashed insistence that it alone will define its national interests. Here the Habermas–Derrida initiative resonated with a long-standing debate about the military–political alliance of Europe and the US. Indeed, Habermas's arguments seemed in some ways to re-work the arguments of a year earlier by Robert Kagan, who famously claimed that Americans were from Mars and Europeans were from Venus when it came to their views on foreign policy. The difference, of course, is that Kagan the neo-conservative, who argued that this distinctiveness was a product of differences in *power*, saw the American stance as positive and even necessary.[5] In contrast, Habermas the social democrat suggested that the divergences were the product of different degrees of *social development* and viewed the European model as preferable.

Underlying these visions are profound historical differences in the political cultures of European nation-states and of the

United States. In his essay, Ulrich Preuss provides an insightful historical overview, noting ~~that the United States has had an historical propensity – in part as a result of its relative geopolitical isolation – to seek 'absolute security,' rather than the 'relative security' with which most countries must be satisfied~~. Aside from those historical considerations, many of the authors seem to agree that Europe should try to be more assertive in its foreign and military policies. The respective positions differ to the extent that some perceive a European power as a counterweight to the power of the United States, whereas others see the enhancement of European military capacity as the basis of even stronger ties with the US. ~~Many of the authors share with the great majority of Europe's political class the view that it is necessary to develop a common European defense and security policy, but that it is not possible or desirable to do this against the United States~~. Moreover, if indeed the rift between the United States and Europe was based on disagreements with a particular administration and not a more deep-rooted anti-Americanism, the tensions that emerged out of the Iraq conflict are temporary, not permanent. Accordingly, Habermas's conception seems ambiguous. Some contributors to the debate argued that he overstated the differences between Europe and the United States. Others have suggested that he did not sufficiently appreciate the extent to which opposition to the war is a function of a strong anti-Americanism rather than of sincere engagement with the issues at hand. ~~Ironically, the very opposition of Europeans to the United States seems to be based on two shared premises: namely that only the US can be an effective military power, and that both sides are demanding that Europe shore up its military capacity, even if both sides recognize that Europe is unlikely to match the military prowess of the US~~.

However, here too the focus on transatlantic relations seems to be more about how to transform a balance of national foreign policy interests in Europe into one consolidated voice. The reluctance to partake in the Iraqi war was not only a function of principled concerns with sovereignty and doubts about the potential threat and unilateral action; it was also the result of divergent foreign policy and economic interests among EU countries. These positions were also based on distinctive, long-standing interests and economic considerations that arose out of the preferred trading status that the UN-sponsored embargo of Iraq afforded to France, Russia, and other countries. The question of how to design a joint foreign policy that would be based on a consensual view among all Union members remained unresolved. Or rather, transatlantic tensions and the accompanying divisions within a Europe caught up in the stresses of 'enlargement' have thrown into sharp relief the distance from the old consensual model of the smaller European Community.

Core Europe

Ultimately the transatlantic strains served as a mirror for internal European fault lines that were surfacing as the Union faced the imminent inclusion of ten new members. The intra-'Western' *querelles* can thus be seen as a displaced version of internal power struggles within the various bodies of the EU as well as part of a renewed effort to tackle the 'identity deficit' that continues to plague Europe. What is striking about the reactions to the notion of 'core Europe' is the fact that collective identifications remain up for grabs. Here it is noticeable that few of the authors are suggesting national alternatives. They might not like what they see, but their responses involve largely non-national alternatives.

Hence an issue that raised passionate reactions was the very notion of a 'core Europe.' Habermas's choice of this term is noteworthy, given its political provenance: The term 'Kerneuropa' was originally coined in 1994, in a highly influential policy paper written by Karl Lamers,[6] then foreign policy spokesman for Germany's center-right Christian Democratic Union (CDU), together with Wolfgang Schäuble, then the CDU's chairman.[7] The 'Schäuble–Lamers Paper' had appealed

[handwritten marginalia: Belgiu... Lux. Nederlandos.]

to a 'core Europe' – Germany, France, and the Benelux countries – as the motor for the ongoing project of economic and political integration of the European Union. The levels of economic and political integration already achieved in this 'core' of EU member states, the paper argued, could be tapped as a resource for further integration only by conceiving of a 'multi-speed Europe'; that is, a European core with highly accelerated and intensive integration in areas such as monetary union, taxation, and social welfare policies. The tempo and intensity of integration in the core countries could generate momentum to continue on to other, non-economic areas for integration such as security and defense policies and foreign policy, and this internal, high-speed integration would, in turn, provide the impetus for integration with and among the other EU member-states, whose integration dynamic could proceed more slowly and deliberately.

From the beginning the Schäuble-Lamers proposal for a core-periphery model or 'two-speed Europe' was controversial, with many objecting that the notion introduced an unnecessary division between a European avant-garde and the majority of EU member-states, which were consigned to second-class status – a worry that seemed confirmed, albeit indirectly, in the division of EU states in their position on the Iraq war that was caricatured in US Secretary of Defense Donald Rumsfeld's dismissal of Germany and France as 'old Europe.' But the idea of a European 'core' capable of expanding its global influence on the basis of accelerated integration was also attractive beyond the CDU. Not just intellectuals such as Habermas but also Joschka Fischer, leader of the German Green party and highly visible Foreign Minister in Germany's current 'Red-Green' coalition government, adopted the 'core Europe' concept as a means for expressing the need to continue the project of European integration beyond the economic and financial realms and toward a political or even a 'normative' integration. While Fischer has since publicly abandoned the 'core Europe' conception in favor of a more inclusive plan for political integration in the European Union, it lies at the heart of Habermas's vision of a Europe that 'speaks with one voice.'

What role this highly contested notion of core Europe continues to play in Habermas's position remains a sore point for many intellectuals who responded to the manifesto.[8] Some of the commentators viewed Habermas's conception of Europe as too narrow, reflecting primarily the experiences of France and Germany. Others saw his position as emblematic of a mentality that suited the old (i.e., pre-1989) Federal Republic. Zeroing in on one of the more perplexing facets of the 'manifesto,' Timothy Garton Ash and Ralf Dahrendorf began their 'Reply to Habermas' with the words, 'one might think that we are experiencing a renaissance of Gaullism.' Habermas insisted, however, that the point was not to promote a 'two-speed' Europe, but simply to push the process of integration faster than was occurring up till the time of his initiative.

European Identity and the Role of the Constitutive Other

What is a European identity? What should it consist of? How can it accommodate the differences between nations? These and many related questions about the possibilities of creating a supra-national mode of identification are at the center of an enterprise that recognizes the limitation of a utilitarian focus on economic cooperation.[9] It is not only the disdain for Eurocrats but also the fact that economic relations in the context of expansion have become the subject of tense intra-European conflicts that convey a sense of urgency about the need to establish cultural commonalities. Here Europe finds itself in a continuous tension between the desire to replicate the national experience that looks toward shared pasts (depending on whom you ask, they can be based on geography, values, religion, history, and so on) and the recognition that binding such pasts into a unified frame of reference complicates matters. Claus Offe has suggested a key reason why 'Europe' has failed to capture the emotional attachment of its member-citizens: namely, because the European Union lacks the crucial element of liberation – whether from an illegitimate form of political rule or from external domination – that has typically given rise to the birth of new states. To the extent that people cannot envision the completion of European unification as *liberation*, their enthusiasm is likely to be restrained.[10]

On an official level, the tendency is to look toward the future. The design of the euro with its neutral symbols of bridges and other links is one example. Examining textbook representations, Yasemin Soysal has shown that Europeanness is not addressed in terms of origins, or through religious and ethnic narratives, but more in abstract universal principles. The balance between universalism and particularism as well as the particular quality of universalism, as it were, are part of this discussion. Thus, for instance, Habermas's suggestion that February 15 constitutes the birthday of a *European* public sphere was criticized by some for ignoring the fact that the demonstrations against the Iraq war were in fact *worldwide*.[11] Universalistic principles and ideals cannot be confined to Europe or its member-states. 'This is what makes it impossible to define a territorially and culturally bounded European identity. But this is also what makes a European identity possible; one that transcends Europe and is legitimated by claims to universality rather than particularisms. This Europe does not exist against its "others".'[12] One might call this the 'Europe of the textbooks.'

The Europe of the manifesto – the one that is engaged in a heated debate about its short-lived multicultural policies and demographic transformations (a euphemism for the growing presence of non-Christians, and more specifically Muslims) – seems more intent on looking at the cohesive functions of boundary maintenance, both literally and culturally. The idea of 'Fortress Europe' has long since entered into mainstream policies on immigration. Figuratively, globalization has become a source of nostalgic retreat for many. Is the transatlantic rift or the anti-American perception of core-Europeans also a reflection of a habit that requires a constitutive other? After all, for a long time the Iron Curtain served an important political–cultural function. Now the 'threat' is more amorphous and comes in the form of globalization and other unknown forces. Culturally speaking the United States seems to function as a substitute for the negative effects of a globalizing world. Globalization is frequently perceived as Americanization. References to the US often seem to serve the role of Europe's new constitutive other. On a deeper, cultural level, the transatlantic tensions are also a function of competing conceptions of universalism. The European insistence on being a particular project based on a collective memory of universalist values clashes with the universal mission of the US and growing global resistance to a universalism perceived as a Western imposition, as suggested in recent debates about the distinctive forms of 'human rights' and 'democracy.'

'Competing Traditions'

However, this 'constitutive other' is not just coming from the outside but is already inside or about to join the Union. One refers to Europe's growing Islamic population, the other to the new members from Eastern and Central Europe. The Eastern European responses to Habermas's idea of a core Europe were particularly passionate. This has less to do with Habermas's intentions and everything to do with the reality of the unification process. Having had to fulfill a long list of political and economic conditions to join the EU, as well as partake in more recent negotiations over full freedom for labor to move across Europe, the new member-states have a sense of being second-class citizens in the European project. Together with the failure to agree on a constitution (and with it, the absence of a 'constitutional moment')[13] this perception has raised a host of concerns among the new members. Ultimately, the idealization of Europe (which for many people still means Western Europe), and its mythological proportions cultivated under Communism and behind an Iron Curtain, are now exposed to transitional moments that require adjustments and invite disillusionment and simple disappointment about unfulfilled expectations.

Similarly, ~~many East Europeans have more positive – if perhaps also idealized – views about 'America' than do West Europeans~~. Whereas West Europeans seem often quite unaware of the fact that the Marshall Plan and American military might allowed them to recover from the self-inflicted carnage of the Second World War, the ~~East Europeans tend to be more appreciative of the United States' role in opposing and defeating Communism~~. After all, unlike their counterparts in the West, East Europeans actually had to endure the oppression and privation of Soviet domination. Their nostalgia for the period before 1989, which Garton Ash and Dahrendorf observed in Habermas's manifesto, thus tends to be distinctly limited.

A sense of Europeanness or of being part of Europe is frequently a function of where one is going, so to speak. Thus Poles, Czechs, Hungarians, and others have long been Europeans, particularly when leaving the continent. Being from Europe and returning to it from the US, for instance, one inevitably becomes European (as Americans draw few distinctions among the different European nations, Donald Rumsfeld notwithstanding). Incidentally, the new Central and Eastern European member-states also resent the fact that they are lumped together at the same time that, faced with the dominant and dominating West, they are also cultivating their own traditions. After all, the Central European contribution to core European values (especially in the cultural and artistic fields) has a long tradition. With the demise of Communism, this old tradition has resurfaced, partly out of choice and partly in response to the somewhat arrogant conduct of their Western European neighbors. Now that the old Hapsburg Empire has been integrated into the European project, East European intellectuals and politicians self-consciously draw on its heritage. To be sure, there is a difference between this cultural vestige and the amalgam of countries that have become part of the political Central European Initiative. ~~The main point, however, is the fact that, for them, Europe carries pre-Second World War associations evoking images from the past.~~ For Western

Europeans it is a future-oriented project that, in many ways, seeks to put the tormented European past behind it. In short, for 'old' Europeans, Europe is the future, whereas for 'new' Europeans, it is the past.

Not that Western Europeans aren't also looking into certain aspects of their past to sharpen a sense of commonality (see for example the sanitized narration of the Vikings as benevolent merchants, or repeated references to Europe's 'Judeo-Christian' roots). However, they pay less attention to the cultural influences of their new neighbors, whose experience was always shaped by their proximity to the Balkans, Byzantium, and the Mediterranean. How difficult those multiple references, pasts, and exposures can be is well illustrated in the heated debate about Turkey's admission into the EU. These and related anxieties have heightened with the prospect of unification in the context of globalization. And in good old European fashion, the problem has been shifted onto 'others' – the US from outside, and immigrants (and Muslims) from inside.

Some contributors suggested that Habermas had failed to appreciate the proper role of religion in a number of European countries not currently in the Union, or even within 'core Europe.' Religious and ethnic differences may well turn out to be a crucial obstacle. The community of Christianity might serve as a buzzword, but the schism between Western Latin-Roman and Eastern Greek Orthodox Christianity remains resilient. Many of these countries have a long history of being torn between the West and the East. Subject to Soviet anti-Western rhetoric during the Cold War, frequently abandoned by the West in their struggle to free themselves from the shackles of totalitarian regimes (Poland's 'Solidarity' is a case in point), many of these Central European countries have developed cautious attitudes.

After the war in Iraq shifted from a 'hot' to a 'lukewarm' phase, efforts to patch up the unsettled European–American relationship were apparent on both sides. Conciliatory gestures were made, especially involving France and Germany. Similarly, the United States increasingly recognized that, in order to have an effective transfer of power to the Iraqis, it needed both other national allies and the United Nations, whose authorization and assistance it had previously spurned. As signs of a rapprochement mounted, a tragic explosion in Spain killed nearly two hundred people in the immediate run-up to national elections. As no group immediately took responsibility for the attack, a period of acrimonious uncertainty ensued. When the Socialists unexpectedly beat the party of strong US ally José María Aznar and replaced him in the prime minister's office with José Luis Rodríguez Zapatero, some cried 'appeasement' and saw the vote as widening the Atlantic once again. Instead, while Zapatero has said clearly that he thought the Iraq war had made the West more unsafe, and that he would withdraw Spanish troops from the country, he also acted to reassure the United States that Spain was a reliable ally by indicating that Spanish troops would remain if the Iraqi occupation received a UN mandate. Still, Zapatero has also argued that his government's aim is 'to forge a common European foreign policy to counterbalance the power of the United States.'[14] The new Spanish prime minister's statement of his government's policy indicates clearly the persistence of the division within the West, despite recent hints of a reconciliation, and the resiliency of the basic idea behind Habermas's argument for a 'core Europe.'

These developments are accompanied by an inward shift toward concerns about migrants and heated debates about the 'Islamic Question,' exacerbated by the fallout from '3/11.' Themes of religious tolerance, multiculturalism, separation of state and mosque (despite the fact that the discussion is one of principle, it appears clearly directed toward Europe's large community of Muslims), and the tension between human rights and anti-terror policies have recently shifted the discussion back to a European terrain.

Suffice it to say that the rifts and divergences between Europe and the United States that were bared during the Iraq war have a durable significance. The series of interventions initiated by

Jürgen Habermas, and his essay with Jacques Derrida in particular, ~~point to the urgency of the issue of European–American
understandings of each other~~. The responses reveal the range
of positions toward this set of issues of some of Europe's leading
political intellectuals. Their contributions frame a debate that
is likely to remain with us for a long time to come. Despite
the occasionally acrimonious criticisms, the discussion itself
bears witness to the vibrancy and the importance of a transatlantic public sphere.

The Editors

August 2004

---

[1] The term 'constitutional patriotism' (*Verfassungspatriotismus*) was originally coined by German political theorist Dolf Sternberger (see Dolf
Sternberger, *Verfassungspatriotismus. Schriften, Band X* [Frankfurt am
Main: Suhrkamp Verlag, 1990]). For Habermas's version of constitutional patriotism, see his essay 'Struggles for Recognition in the
Democratic Constitutional State,' in *The Inclusion of the Other. Studies
in Political Theory* (Cambridge, MA: MIT Press, 1998), pp. 225–6.

[2] For a good overview of arguments against constitutional patriotism,
and its alternatives, see Craig Calhoun, 'Constitutional Patriotism and
the Public Sphere: Interests, Identity, and Solidarity in the Integration
of Europe,' in Pablo De Greiff and Ciaran Cronin (eds), *Global Justice
and Transnational Politics* (Cambridge, MA: MIT Press, 2002),
pp. 275–312.

[3] Dominique Strauss-Kahn, 'Die Geburt einer Nation,' in *Frankfurter
Rundschau*, March 11, 2003.

[4] The quotations are, of course, from Jefferson's 'Declaration of
Independence,' in Merrill Peterson (ed.), *The Portable Thomas Jefferson*
(New York: Viking, 1975), p. 235.

[5] The dynamic character of the ongoing discussion about the transatlantic relationship is evidenced in the gradual shift in tone that has
emerged in relations between the US administration and its European
counterparts. For example, it was clear during German Chancellor
Gerhard Schröder's visit to Washington in early 2004 that both
Germany and the US were eager to mend fences. There are various
motivations for this change. One striking element, however, relates to
the recognition that even a superpower like the US must take aspects
of 'soft power' into consideration. Thus, the same Kagan who previously celebrated American power and ridiculed European weakness
subsequently stressed that the struggle for international legitimacy

remains a central element of political success (see Robert Kagan, 'A Tougher War For The US Is One Of Legitimacy,' *New York Times*, Op-Ed, January 24, 2004).

[6] Karl Lamers (1994), 'Strengthening the Hard Core,' in Peter Gowan and Perry Anderson (eds), *The Question of Europe* (London: Verso, 2000), pp. 104–16.

[7] As it happens, Habermas would share the stage with Schäuble at an event to discuss the 'core Europe' initiative that took place at Muschg's Academy of Arts in Berlin in late June 2003; see Seibt below.

[8] To be sure, this is not a new debate as every round of membership extension has raised questions about the vision of Europe. See Perry Anderson (1996), 'The Europe to Come,' in Gowan and Anderson (eds), *The Question of Europe*, pp. 126–45.

[9] And it has been a question that has accompanied the formation of the EU since its inception. See Anthony D. Smith (1992), 'National Identity and European Unity,' in Gowan and Anderson (eds), *The Question of Europe*, pp. 318–42. In the same volume, J.G.A. Pocock (1991), 'Deconstructing Europe,' pp. 297–317 .

[10] See Claus Offe, 'Sozialpolitik und internationale Politik: Über zwei Hindernisse auf dem Wege zum "Zusammenhalt" Europas,' unpublished manuscript of a lecture given in Madrid, October 2003.

[11] This broader and more inclusive perspective is also reflected in the rhetoric of the anti-war movement, which has self-consciously drawn on February 15 – and, more recently, the anniversary of demonstrations on March 20, 2003 — by emphasizing the globally (albeit mostly Western) coordinated nature of this movement.

[12] Yasemin Soysal, 'European Identity and Narratives of Projection,' paper presented at the conference 'Whose Europe? National Models and the Constitution of the European Union,' Oxford University, April 25–7, 2003.

[13] On October 2004, the member states of the European Union became signatories to the Constitution of Europe. But a long satisfaction process – requiring unanimous endorsement by all 25 member states, and requiring popular referenda in many of them – lies ahead, making the ultimate adoption of the Constitution of Europe far from certain.

[14] Elaine Sciolino, 'Spain's New Leader Blows Both Hot and Cold Toward US,' *New York Times*, national edition, March 22, 2004, p. A3.

1

THE INITIAL SALVOS, MAY 31, 2003

FEBRUARY 15, OR, WHAT BINDS EUROPEANS TOGETHER:
Plea for a Common Foreign Policy, Beginning in Core Europe

Jürgen Habermas and Jacques Derrida

It is the wish of Jacques Derrida and Jürgen Habermas to be co-signatories of what is both an analysis and an appeal. They regard it as both necessary and urgent that French and German philosophers lift their voices together, whatever disagreements may have separated them in the past. The following text was composed by Jürgen Habermas, as will be readily apparent. Though he would have liked to very much, due to personal circumstances Jacques Derrida was unable to compose his own text. Nevertheless, he suggested to Jürgen Habermas that he be the co-signatory of this appeal, and shares its definitive premises and perspectives; the determination of new European political responsibilities beyond any Eurocentrism; the call for a renewed confirmation and effective transformation of international law and its institutions, in particular the UN; a new conception and a new praxis for the distribution of state authority, etc., according to the spirit, if not the precise sense, that refers back to the Kantian tradition. Moreover, many of Jürgen Habermas's points intersect with ones Jacques Derrida has recently developed in his book, Voyous: Deux essais sur la raison *(Galilée, 2002). Within several days, a book by Jürgen Habermas and Jacques Derrida will appear in the United States, consisting of two conversations which both of them held in New York after September 11, 2002.[1] Despite all the obvious differences in their approaches and arguments, there too their views touch on the future of institutions of international law, and the new tasks for Europe.*

We should not forget two dates: the day the newspapers reported to their astonished readers that the Spanish prime minister had invited those European nations willing to support the Iraq war to swear an oath of loyalty to George W. Bush, an invitation issued behind the backs of the other countries of the European Union. But we should also remember the 15th of February 2003, as mass demonstrations in London and Rome, Madrid and Barcelona, Berlin and Paris reacted to this sneak attack. The simultaneity of these overwhelming demonstrations – the largest since the end of the Second World War – may well, in hindsight, go down in history as a sign of the birth of a European public sphere.

During the leaden months prior to the outbreak of the war in Iraq, a morally obscene division of labor provoked strong emotions. The large-scale logistical operation of ceaseless military preparation and the hectic activity of humanitarian aid organizations meshed together as precisely as the teeth of a gear. Moreover, the spectacle took place undisturbed before the eyes of the very population that – robbed of their own initiative – was to be victimized. The precautionary mustering of relief workers, services, and supplies was cloaked in the rash rhetoric of alleviating suffering yet to be inflicted, and reconstructing cities and administrations yet to be ruined. Like searchlights, they picked out the civilized barbarism of coolly planned death (of how many victims?), of torments long since totted up (of how many injured and mutilated, how many thirsty and hungry?), of the long-planned destruction (of how many residential districts and hospitals, how many houses, museums, and markets?). As the war finally began, the Ernst Jünger[2] aesthetic of the skyline of nighttime Baghdad, illuminated by countless explosions, seemed almost harmless.

A Common European Foreign Policy: Who First?

There is no doubt that the power of emotions has brought European citizens jointly to their feet. Yet at the same time, the war made Europeans conscious of the failure of their common foreign policy, a failure that has been a long time in the making. As in the rest of the world, the impetuous break with international law has ignited a debate over the future of the international order in Europe as well. But here, the divisive arguments have cut deeper, and have caused familiar fault lines to emerge even more sharply. Controversies over the role of the American superpower, a future world order, and the relevance of international law and the United Nations all have caused latent contradictions to break out into the open. The gap has grown deeper between continental and Anglo-American countries on the one side, and 'Old Europe' and the Central and Eastern European candidates for entry into the European Union on the other.

In Great Britain, while the special relationship with the United States is by no means uncontested, the priorities of Downing Street are still quite clear. And the Central and Eastern European countries, while certainly working hard for their admission into the EU, are nevertheless not yet ready to place limits on the sovereignty that they have so recently regained. The Iraq crisis was only a catalyst. In the Brussels constitutional convention, there is now a visible contrast between the nations that really want a stronger EU, and those with an *understandable* interest in freezing, or at best cosmetically changing, the existing mode of intergovernmental governance. This contradiction can no longer be finessed. The future constitution will grant us a European foreign minister. But what good is a new political office if governments don't unify in a common policy? A Fischer with a changed job description would remain as powerless as Solana.[3]

For the moment, only the core European nations are ready to endow the EU with certain qualities of a state. But what happens if these countries are able to agree only on a definition of 'self-interest'? If Europe is not to fall apart, these countries will have to make use of the mechanisms for 'strengthened cooperation' mandated by the EU conference at Nice, as a way of taking a first step toward a common foreign policy, a common security policy, and a common defense policy. Only such a step will succeed in generating the momentum that other member-states – initially in the euro zone – will not be able to resist in the long run. In the framework of the future European constitution, there can and must be no separatism. Taking a leading role does not mean excluding. The avant-gardist core of Europe must not wall itself off into a new 'Small Europe.' It must – as it has so often – be the locomotive. It is their own self-interest, to be sure, that will cause the more closely-cooperating member states of the EU to hold the door open. And the probability that the invited states will pass through that door will increase the more capable the core of Europe becomes in effective action externally, and the sooner it can prove that in a complex global society, it's not just divisions that count, but also the soft power of negotiating agendas, relations, and economic advantages.

In this world, the reduction of politics to the stupid and costly alternative of war or peace simply doesn't pay. At the international level and in the framework of the UN, Europe has to throw its weight on the scales to counterbalance the hegemonic unilateralism of the United States. At global economic summits and in the institutions of the WTO, the World Bank, and the IMF, it should exert its influence in shaping the design for a coming global domestic policy.

Political projects that aim at the further development of the EU are now colliding with the limits of the medium of administrative steering. Until now, the functional imperatives for the construction of a common market and the euro zone have driven reforms. These driving forces are now exhausted. A *transformative* politics, which would demand that member states not just overcome obstacles for competitiveness, but form a common will, must connect with the motives and the attitudes of *the citizens themselves*. The legitimacy of majority decisions on highly consequential foreign policies has to rest on a basis of solidarity of out-voted minorities. But this presupposes a feeling of common political belonging on both sides. The population must so to speak 'build up' their national identities, and add to them a European dimension. What is already a fairly abstract form of civic solidarity, still largely confined to members of nation-states, must be extended to include the European citizens of other nations as well.

This raises the question of 'European identity.' Only the consciousness of a shared political fate, and the prospect of a common future, can halt out-voted minorities from obstructing a majority will. The citizens of one nation must regard the citizens of another nation as fundamentally 'one of us.' This desideratum leads to the question that so many sceptics have called attention to: are there historical experiences, traditions, and achievements offering European citizens the consciousness of a shared political fate *that can be shaped together*? An attractive, indeed an infectious 'vision' for a future Europe will not emerge from thin air. At present it can arise only from the disquieting perception of perplexity. But it can well emerge from the difficulties of a situation into which we Europeans have been cast. And it must be articulated from out of the wild cacophony of a multi-vocal public sphere. If this theme has so far not even got on to the agenda, it is we intellectuals who have failed.

The Treacheries of a European Identity

It's easy to find unity without commitment. The image of a peaceful, cooperative Europe, open toward other cultures and capable of dialogue, floats like a mirage before all of us. We welcome the Europe that found exemplary solutions for two problems during the second half of the twentieth century. The EU already offers itself as a form of 'governance beyond the nation-state,' which could set a precedent in the post-national constellation. And for decades European social welfare systems served as a model. Certainly, they have now been thrown on the defensive at the level of the national state. Yet future political efforts at the domestication of global capitalism must not fall below the standards of social justice that they established.

If Europe has solved two problems of this magnitude, why shouldn't it issue a further challenge: to defend and promote a cosmopolitan order on the basis of international law, against competing visions?

Such a Europe-wide discourse, of course, would have to link up with already-existing attitudes, as a stimulus for a process of self-understanding. Two facts would seem to contradict this bold assumption. Haven't the most significant historical achievements of Europe forfeited their identity-forming power precisely through the fact of their worldwide success? And what could hold together a region characterized more than any other by the ongoing rivalries between self-conscious nations?

Insofar as Christianity and capitalism, natural science and technology, Roman law and the Code Napoléon, the bour-geois-urban form of life, democracy and human rights, the secularization of state and society have spread across other continents, these legacies no longer constitute a *proprium*. The Western mind, rooted in the Judeo-Christian tradition, certainly has its characteristic features. But the nations of Europe also share this mental *habitus*, characterized by individ-ualism, rationalism, and activism, with the United States, Canada, and Australia. The 'West' as a spiritual form encom-passes more than just Europe. Moreover, Europe is composed of nation-states that delimit one another polemically. National consciousness, formed by national languages, national liter-atures, and national histories, has long operated as an explosive force.

However, in reaction to the destructive power of this nation-alism, values and habits have also developed which have given contemporary Europe, in its incomparably rich cultural divers-ity, its own face. This is how Europe at large presents itself to non-Europeans. A culture which for centuries has been beset more than any other culture by conflicts between town and country, sacred and secular authorities, by the competition between faith and knowledge, the struggle between states and antagonistic classes, has had to painfully learn how differences can be communicated, contradictions institutionalized, and tensions stabilized. The acknowledgement of differences – the reciprocal acknowledgement of the Other in her otherness – can also become a feature of a common identity.

The pacification of class conflicts within the welfare state, and the self-limitation of state sovereignty in the framework of the EU, are only the most recent examples of this. In the third quarter of the twentieth century, Europe on this side of the Iron Curtain experienced its 'golden age,' as Eric Hobsbawm has called it. Since then, features of a common political mentality have taken shape, so that others often recognize us as Europeans rather than as Germans or French – and that happens not just in Hong Kong, but even in Tel Aviv. And isn't it true? In European societies, secularization is relatively developed. Citizens here regard transgressions of the border between politics and religion with suspicion. Europeans have a relatively large amount of trust in the organizational and steering capacities of the state, while remaining sceptical toward the achievements of markets. They possess a keen sense of the 'dialectic of enlightenment'; they have no naively optimistic expectations about technological progress. They maintain a preference for the welfare state's guarantees of social security and for regulations on the basis of solidarity. The threshold of tolerance for the use of force against persons is relatively low. The desire for a multilateral and legally regulated international order is connected with the hope for an effective global domestic policy, within the framework of a reformed United Nations.

The fortunate historical constellation in which West Europeans developed this kind of mentality in the shadow of the Cold War has changed since 1989–90. But February 15 shows that the mentality has survived the context from which it sprang. This also explains why 'old Europe' sees itself challenged by the blunt hegemonic politics of its ally. And why so many in Europe who welcome the fall of Saddam as an act of liberation also reject the illegality of the unilateral, pre-emptive and deceptively justified invasion. But how stable is this mentality? Does it have roots in deeper historical experiences and traditions?

Today we know that many political traditions which command authority through the illusion of 'naturalness' have in fact been 'invented.' By contrast, a European identity born in the daylight of the public sphere would have something constructed about it from the very beginning. But only what is constructed through an arbitrary choice carries the stigma of randomness. The political–ethical will that drives the hermeneutics of processes of self-understanding is not arbitrary. Distinguishing between the legacy we appropriate, and the one we want to refuse, demands just as much circumspection as the decision about the interpretation through which we appropriate it for ourselves. Historical experiences are only *candidates* for a self-conscious appropriation; without such a self-conscious act they cannot attain the power to shape our identity. To conclude, a few notes on such 'candidates' that might help the European postwar consciousness gain a sharper profile.

Historical Roots of a Political Profile

In modern Europe, the relation between church and state developed differently on either side of the Pyrenees, differently north and south of the Alps, west and east of the Rhine. In different European countries, the idea of the state's neutrality in relation to different world-views has assumed different legal forms. And yet within civil society, religion overall assumes a comparably un-political position. We may have cause to regret this social *privatization of faith* in other respects, but it has desirable consequences for our political culture. For us, a president who opens his daily business with public prayer, and associates his significant political decisions with a divine mission, is hard to imagine.

Civil society's emancipation from the protection of an absolutist regime was not connected everywhere in Europe with the democratic appropriation and transformation of the modern administrative state. But the spread of the ideals of the French

Revolution throughout Europe explains, among other things, why politics in both of its forms – as organizing power and as a medium for the institutionalization of political liberty – has been welcomed in Europe. By contrast, the triumph of capitalism was bound up with sharp class conflicts, and this fact has hindered an equally positive appraisal of free markets. That differing evaluation of *politics* and *market* may explain Europeans' trust in the civilizing power of the state, and their expectations for its capacity to correct 'market failures.'

The party system that emerged from the French Revolution has often been copied. But only in Europe does this system also serve an ideological competition that subjects the socio-pathological results of capitalist modernization to an ongoing political evaluation. This fosters the sensitivity of citizens to the paradoxes of progress. The contest between conservative, liberal, and socialist agendas comes down to the weighing of two aspects: Do the benefits of a chimerical progress outweigh the losses that come with the disintegration of protective, traditional forms of life? Or do the benefits that today's processes of 'creative destruction' promise for tomorrow outweigh the pain of modernity's losers?

In Europe, those who have been affected by class distinctions, and their enduring consequences, understood these burdens as a fate that can be averted only through collective action. In the context of workers' movements and the Christian socialist traditions, an ethics of solidarity, the struggle for 'more social justice', with the goal of equal provision for all, asserted itself against the individualistic ethos of market justice that accepts glaring social inequalities as part of the bargain.

Contemporary Europe has been shaped by the experience of the totalitarian regimes of the twentieth century and by the Holocaust – the persecution and the annihilation of European Jews in which the National Socialist regime made the societies of the conquered countries complicit as well. Self-critical controversies about this past remind us of the moral basis of politics. A heightened sensitivity to injuries to personal and bodily integrity reflects itself, among other ways, in the fact that both the Council of Europe and EU made the ban on capital punishment a condition for membership.

A bellicose past once entangled all European nations in bloody conflicts. They drew a conclusion from that military and spiritual mobilization against one another: the imperative of developing new, supranational forms of cooperation after the Second World War. The successful history of the European Union may have confirmed Europeans in their belief that the domestication of state power demands a *mutual* limitation of sovereignty, on the global as well as the nation-state level.

Each of the great European nations has experienced the bloom of its imperial power. And, what in our context is more important still, each has had to work through the experience of the loss of its empire. In many cases this experience of decline was associated with the loss of colonial territories. With the growing distance of imperial domination and the history of colonialism, the European powers also got the chance for reflexive distance from themselves. They could learn from the perspective of the defeated to perceive themselves in the dubious role of victors who are called to account for the violence of a forcible and uprooting process of modernization. This could support the rejection of Eurocentrism, and inspire the Kantian hope for a global domestic policy.

Frankfurter Allgemeine Zeitung and *Libération*
Translated by Max Pensky

---

1 The book has since appeared: Giovanna Borradori (ed.), *Philosophy in a Time of Terror: Dialogues with Jürgen Habermas and Jacques Derrida* (Chicago: University of Chicago Press, 2003).

2 Ernst Jünger (1895–1998); German writer whose glorification of war (specifically the frontline experience of the First World War) was much admired by Nazis.

3 Javier Solana, formerly the Secretary General of NATO, is High Representative of the European Union's Common Foreign and Security

Policy – in effect the EU's foreign minister. Much criticism has been levelled at the evident lack of influence and political power invested in the office. Joschka Fischer, Germany's popular foreign minister, has been mentioned frequently as a candidate to head a new and presumably expanded EU foreign ministry, though Fischer himself has disavowed any such ambitions.

AN UNCERTAIN EUROPE BETWEEN REBIRTH AND DECLINE

Umberto Eco

This article does not stem from my own initiative. A few weeks ago, Jürgen Habermas contacted a number of colleagues from various European countries and asked each of them to contribute an article. All these articles were to appear on the same day in major European newspapers. Except for some messages in which Habermas explained his intentions, at this very moment I don't know exactly what Habermas and Jacques Derrida (in a joint article that will appear at the same time in the *Frankfurter Allgemeine* and in *Libération*), Fernando Savater (*El País*), Gianni Vattimo (*La Stampa*), Adolf Muschg (*Neue Zürcher Zeitung*), and Richard Rorty (as an overseas contributor, whose article will appear in the *Süddeutsche Zeitung*) are going to write. It may be that the various interventions will spur further discussion. What Habermas asked of his friends and colleagues was to voice the opinion of some European citizens on the current situation of the Union, and to send a series of requests to the national governments as well as to the existing (though not yet fully developed) European government.

This seems to be the least opportune time to make predictions about the future of a united Europe: if anything, the various positions taken with regard to the Iraq war have exposed sharp divisions within Europe. The entry into the Union of some Eastern European nations has drawn together age-old democracies partly willing to put their national sovereignty into question with more recent democracies that aim at strengthening their newly-achieved national sovereignty even at the cost of embarking upon a policy of alliances that goes beyond European borders.

In light of this situation we can say that, on the one hand, a European consciousness and identity does exist, while on the other, a series of events aims at dissolving this very unity.

Here is an example that I know Habermas, too, will use: the fundamental principles of the so-called Western world, the Greek and Judeo-Christian heritage, the ideas of freedom and equality born out of the French Revolution, the heritage of modern science that started with Copernicus, Galileo, Kepler, Descartes, and Francis Bacon, the capitalistic form of production, the secularization of the State, Roman or Common Law, the very idea of justice achieved through class struggle (all typical products of the European Western world, and we could cite many more) are nowadays no longer the exclusive domain of Europe. On the contrary, they have spread and become popular in America, Australia, and – although not everywhere – in many parts of Asia and Africa.

An Uncertain Future Between Rebirth and Decline: The Fate of the Old Continent

Today, Western civilization (a civilization which tends to identify itself with the successful model in the globalization process) no longer coincides with Europe alone.

At the same time, within Western civilization itself we increasingly recognize a European identity. This identity does not emerge so much when we (as Europeans) visit another European country, in which case we tend instead to perceive differences – though they are the same differences that someone from Milan notices when visiting Palermo, or that someone from Calabria notices in Turin. Rather, a European identity reveals itself as soon as we come into contact with a non-European culture, including American culture. There are moments, during a conference, an evening spent among friends from different countries, or even on a sightseeing trip, when we suddenly share a common feeling that makes the behavior and taste of someone from France, Spain, or Germany seem more familiar to us than those of others. Inaugurating a Peace Conference in Paris last December, the French minister and philosopher Luc Ferry observed (his was not a groundbreaking thought, of course, but he nevertheless highlighted it quite powerfully) that today it would be impossible for the French to consider a war against the Germans (and equally inconceivable for the British to imagine waging war against Italy or for the Spanish to invade Flanders), whereas these very conflicts and hostilities that are now relegated to the past had been the norm for two thousand years. This situation is historically new; only fifty years ago it would have been unthinkable. Perhaps we are not always fully conscious of it, but it has come to be inextricably tied to all we do. This is true even for the least cultivated of us Europeans when we go on holiday and, by now carefree and unaware of it, cross a border that our ancestors had approached armed with rifles.

The reasons why a French person may still feel different from a German are countless, but both of them have inherited a series of experiences that have marked them and their respective nations alike: we share a concept of welfare achieved through trade-union struggles as opposed to the homeostasis of the individualistic ethics of success; we all have experienced the failure of colonialism and the loss of our empires; we all have suffered dictatorships, we have known them first-hand, we can recognize their premonitory symptoms, and we have perhaps become (at least for the most part) immune to them. We all have experienced war in our own land, and the state of permanent danger. I daresay that, if two airplanes had crashed into Notre Dame or Big Ben, the reaction would obviously have been one of fear, pain, indignation, but it would not have had the shocking tone and the depression syndrome counterbalanced by the instinct to take immediate, unavoidable action that gripped the Americans, who were hit for the first time in their own land.

Inwardly (between nations) it's hard to find commonality at u.s)
(in europe) Outwardly (look at u.s) it is easy

All in all, Europeans have a lot in common – joy and sorrow, pride and shame, traditions to defend and remorse still to process. Every European country, unlike other countries, has experienced its closeness to Asia or Africa with which it has held relations of trade and/or conflict, but from which it is not separated by oceans. Is this enough to make Europe truly united? Indeed it isn't, and we see this every day, despite the euro and despite the fact that many countries wish to gain access into this community. All seem to want to participate in a union within which they are willing to renounce something but not everything, and within which they are ready to spark new conflicts, as was revealed by their various positions with regard to the Iraq war.

The fact is that the unity Europe cannot find within itself is now imposed upon us by the way matters have evolved. During the Cold War, Europeans, after going through the Second World War (and being divided into East and West), were forced to live under the shield of other world powers, the United States or the Soviet Union. Each of these powers played out its own destiny in Europe. China threatened to become a dreadful adversary of the United States only in the long run, but at the time China was busy struggling to maintain its internal stability, and it had to face directly not the Americans but the Russians. The Americans could sustain a deadlock in Korea and a defeat in Vietnam, but it was in Europe that they played their game, and it was in Europe that they won it, with the collapse of the Soviet empire. Placed in the center of a game too big for them, the European nations had to shape their foreign policy according to one of the two coalitions with which they identified, accepting a unified military defense (NATO or the Warsaw Pact).

demographic deficit = not enough rebirths

The world scenario had already changed after the collapse of the Berlin Wall, but the time of reckoning arrived during the past few years, perhaps since the United States' limited interest in the Balkan question came to light. Having defeated that which had been its enemy for fifty years, the United States realized there was yet another enemy, one with no fixed borders but certainly localizable within the Muslim world, within the Middle and Far East. It is against this enemy that the Americans have directed their military force, from Kabul to Baghdad and perhaps even further. This new war has even pushed them to relocate their military bases; and in any case, NATO is no longer considered reliable (in part because it has become clear that, for historical and geographical reasons, European countries have a relationship to the Arab world which partially clashes with American interests).

In the meantime, it has also become clear that the big confrontation the United States is preparing to face is with China. There is nothing to indicate that it will involve war, but it will certainly be a confrontation in economic and demographic terms. One only needs to visit an American university to realize how many scholarships, research positions, and student leadership roles are increasingly held by Asian students (who, leaving any genetic considerations aside, are culturally much better prepared than their peers of European origin to work eighteen hours a day in order to achieve positions of excellence). American scientific development will rely more and more on the importation not of European but of Asian intellects, from India to China to Japan. This means that American interests in general will shift from the Atlantic to the Pacific, in the same way as the great centers of production and research have long moved to, or have been directly established on, the West Coast. In the long run, New York will become an American Florence, still a centre of fashion and culture, but less and less a place where big decisions are made. The United States is going to become not an Atlantic, but a Pacific country, and for Europe this has a very precise meaning: while the WASPs of the 1920s lived the myth of Paris, the new American VIPs will live in states where the *New York Times* is not even distributed, or it arrives the next day and only in specific areas. They will live in places where Americans will know less and less about Europe, and if they do learn about it, they will fail to understand the reasoning of this exotic continent, much further and much more mysterious than Hawaii or Japan.

With the United States shifting its attention to the Middle East and to the immense universe of the Pacific, Europe might not count anymore. In any case, even those who are most fervently pro-American will have to admit that it would no longer make sense for the United States to worry about a continent which (despite the fact that American roots lie in it – but then again, how many Americans are named Pérez or Chong Li?) is no longer threatened by Nazi tanks or by Cossacks eager to have their horses drink the holy water of St Peter's Cathedral.

Left alone by force of circumstances (as a result of an almost Hegelian rule according to which things happen as rational reality commands), Europe will either become European, or it will fall apart.

The latter hypothesis seems unrealistic, but we may as well trace it: Europe will either become Balkanized, or Latin-Americanized. It will be the new world powers (and perhaps, in a far future, it might be China instead of the United States) that will gamble with the little European countries according to their needs, regardless of whether it might be more convenient for them (and for their survival as world powers) to have bases in Poland or Gibraltar, or perhaps in Helsinki or Tallinn because of the polar routes. And the more Europe will be divided and the euro becomes less competitive in the world markets, the better. After all, one cannot blame a great world power for minding its own interests above all others. Or, alternatively, Europe will find the energy to present itself as the Third Pole between the United States and the Orient (we will see whether the Orient will coincide with Beijing or, who knows, with Tokyo or Singapore). In order to present itself as the third pole, Europe has only one possibility: after achieving a customs union and a monetary union, it will have to devise its own united foreign policy and defense system – even a minimal one, since it would not be reasonable to imagine that Europe might have to invade China or fight against the United States –

sufficient to provide a policy of defense and immediate intervention that NATO can no longer ensure.

Will the European governments be able to reach these agreements? Habermas's appeal suggests that it would be impossible to reach this goal immediately with a broader Europe to include Estonia, Turkey, Poland, and maybe, one day, Russia. However, this plan might appeal to the group of countries that gave birth to the European Union. If a proposal were to stem from that group, little by little the other nations would (perhaps) follow. Is this utopia? Well, common sense dictates that it is a utopia made necessary by the new order of world stability. It is either this way, or no way at all. In order to survive, so to speak, Europe is condemned to find common strategies for foreign policy and defense. Otherwise it will become, no offence to anyone, Guatemala.

This is the meaning of the call some European citizens are addressing to the governments of the continent in which they were born and where they would like to continue living, proud to be part of it.

La Repubblica

'CORE EUROPE':

Thoughts About the European Identity

Adolf Muschg

What lies at the heart of European unity? It is far easier to say what the necessary, though perhaps insufficient, conditions are for a union that will be politically sustainable. With a throw of the dice, monetary union cast mutual interests into the economic arena, where it seems that they can be more firmly established (and measurable).

But the competition for the most favorable price/productivity ratio – in a worldwide market that cannot be limited regionally – does not in itself create any values that Europeans can recognize as their own. That wealthier nations have obligations, even when they lead to competitive disadvantage, has become the guiding star of a different political entity. As a result, social costs are simply written off as deficits that can no longer be afforded. The stability pact which forces social programs to modify their fiscal demands has meanwhile become the true benchmark of Europe's economic capability. But a Europe that has no function beyond bookkeeping loses its basis as a society of solidarity. And when there are no longer any surpluses from which to distribute its wealth, it no can longer offer any compensation to its members. Seen from a purely economic standpoint, the reunification of Germany has since proven to be a bad investment, which has brought the engine of its economic strength to a standstill. That the expansion to the East might prove to be a better deal for Europe is a bold speculation, and, as the Iraq war has mercilessly demonstrated, there is little chance that expansion will result in the political idyll that many had hoped for.

Seeds of Disunity

The 'community of values' of the expanded European Union is dominated by so many diverse priorities that one must fear for the EU's ability to act. The storehouse of hard-won (and correspondingly highly valued) national identities that 'new Europe' brings to the 'old' one stands at odds with Europe's historical achievement, and even here awakens the national-istic-conservative seeds of division.

The 'never again' feeling of a 150-year European Civil War was part of the founding pathos of the Treaty of Rome that brought together both the victors and the defeated of the Second World War. Even if the willingness for peace – in the shadow of the Cold War – was far from unconditional, it never-theless integrated the Germans into an alliance that credibly neutralized their military potential with respect to their neigh-bors. And nobody pursued European integration more assiduously, especially in the form of active reparations, than the West Germans themselves – more vigorously than their NATO membership, which, although assuring a necessary degree of security and freeing the national economy for its postwar economic miracle, did nothing to address a divided national conscience. The twofold trauma of war guilt and the Holocaust came together into a complex of obligatory self-censure that could only be overcome in the higher unity of Europe. For the sake of peace, even the partition of Germany was accepted.

The 'change through dialogue' [*Wandel durch Annäherung*] approach contributed more effectively to the fall of the Wall and to the implosion of the Soviet empire than the 'deploy-ment of new arms,' which was emphatically rejected. This approach was part of the German '*Ostpolitik*' (policy toward the East) since the time of Willy Brandt – a policy to employ utmost caution in disarming potentially explosive historical situations. After the goal had been attained beyond anyone's expectations, it was inevitable that everyone would discover that the clocks of the liberated countries were set to different times. Everywhere where former dissidents came to power, the struggle for human and civil rights, even including the murder of tyrants, was placed above the demands for the maintenance of peace and, amidst the process of their new membership, these new leaders accepted a new division within the EU. For even in the south of Rumsfeld's 'old' Europe the governments agreed with the 'new' ones that a war, even without the blessing of the law of nations, can be waged and may actually be advisable and just. Thus, the Anglo-American unilateralism created a situation in Iraq that paralyzed Europe and brought unexpected coalitions among the states opposing war; i.e., France and Germany, Russia too, and, at an appropriate distance, China.

After the outcome of the war with which we are all familiar, the discussion of which nations now ought to consider themselves 'isolated' seems to have been decided. But doubts emerged about how a significant power might develop that could speak with one voice. Though too large to be a politically mute mass, they remain too disparate to carry their weight in global political terms. As Goethe tells us in his *Wilhelm Meister's Apprenticeship*, 'meaning expands but paralyzes: the deed invigorates, yet limits.' Europe's discovery of the 'limit' of Bush's new world order is no compensation for the failure of the 'meaning' of Europe to coalesce into a unified political will. Giscard d'Estaing's constitutional convention in Brussels will never achieve its ends so long as the true constitution of the Europeans leaves him dangling in the air. If, however, the lowest common denominator of Europe cannot be the economy, and the greatest, i.e., the culture of Europe, remains nothing more than an image painted in the heavens of political speeches, then on what should the unity of Europe be founded?

The question of Europe is akin to St Augustine's question regarding the nature of time: As long as he was not asked what it is supposed to be, he knew what it was; if he was asked, however, he didn't know what it was at all. Thus the answer could simply be that Europe is a reality that comes into being simply by virtue of the fact that it is created. With the caveat (not unfamiliar to the Swiss) that what is created is also what is desired. Undoubtedly, Europe exists only as a community of memories and experiences, but with the peculiarity that these are memories that had to separate us thoroughly enough before they united us, and that the experiences were those of differences that seemed insurmountable. And yet they have been overcome, though not by those who acted deliberately, but by those who were profoundly disturbed.

As a Swiss European, the German–French reconciliation remains for me more of a genuine miracle than the end of the Cold War. The core of the old Europe was a division that became the outline of a new division. In the middle of historical battlefields, from Brussels by way of Luxembourg to Strasbourg, the EU capitals are located like the sutures in a wound that must never re-open. This core Europe has learned to make peace with itself, *à tout prix*; for the price paid for it remains an enduring obligation of Europe and to Europe.

✗ Core Achievement

One wishes that from this an exemplary cure will come: one that would also serve as a model for filling in trenches, and gradually dismantling the walls along the wide-open eastern borders of Eastern Europe – wide open in more than one sense. But, since wishful thinking does not help, the cohesion of core Europe, and its ideal of *acquis communautaire*,[1] cannot be arbitrarily put to the test. What has been achieved in the West in terms of the civilizing of politics must remain inalienable. And in borderline cases, which no European would wish for, retreating into a shell is only appropriate when a resolute historical will has effectively defeated the idiocy of nationalism – my country: right or wrong. This, the core achievement of the coming Europe, can certainly still be lost. Traces of the Iron Curtain still intimidate Europe even after the inhuman border fortifications have been torn down. The spread of nationalistic, populist reaction on both sides of the former border proves that the wounds inflicted by totalitarianism still remain infected. As the thawing of the old blocs wanes, the anesthesia with which those subjected to its logic were compulsorily pacified and their nationality made invisible also fades; now they imperiously demand the return of their rights. And while it may be historically and culturally valid to claim that Europe lives from its contradictions, European politics cannot abide any thoughtless contradictions. It must take care of this threat institutionally. Because what enables the Europeans to work with each other and with themselves is so precious that it must be bearable and must be sustained and preserved in an effective federal body.

In many respects, the European process today resembles the one that Switzerland underwent between the 1818 and 1848 Congresses of Vienna. Twenty-two stubbornly independent political communities, each of them politically labile and hardly any of them with a stable political status, achieved a viable working relationship in order to harvest the fruit of their (always defined as European) differences in the form of a confederation. The new federal authorities were aware of the fact that they had to govern a political system composed entirely of minority states, while at the same time reconciling them with one another. For its part, the EU does not benefit from two of the advantages enjoyed by the Swiss in their unification process: the insignificance of Switzerland's political power and its commitment to neutrality in foreign affairs. A global player such as the EU cannot hide; it is however alerted and made cautious through its own contradictions and will have to develop a special sensitivity for the contradictions of others. If it does not 'learn how to win' from the USA, it will be because it had to learn to weigh the price paid by the victors. 'One more victory like that and I will be lost,' said the ancient King Pyrrhus; the Europeans had to pay so high a price for their victories that they are no longer willing to 'win' even the presumably final victory. Their experience tells them that today the 'war against terrorism' produces more enemies than it can conquer and therefore has to count among the very enemies that that war pledges to eradicate. The Crusades of the past originated in Europe and so it is no longer willing to have anything to do with such things. Yet even to control them, it will still need soldiers; radical pacifism would be anything but a guarantee of peace. The unity of Switzerland in the nineteenth century was in practice shaped more through its army than through its patriotic rhetoric. Europe's foreign affairs will need a face such as that of Joschka Fischer, whose biography offers a kind of guarantee that both sides of any issue will be heard, and that the maxim 'The greater the enemy, the greater the honor' has had its day as Europe's motto.

Sharing a Common Destiny

What holds Europe together and what divides it are at heart the same thing: common memories and habits, acquired step by step through the process of distancing oneself from fatal habits. Europe is what Europe is becoming. It is neither the Occident nor the cradle of civilization; it does not have a monopoly on science, enlightenment, and modernity. It shouldn't attempt to ground its identity in any other way than through its own experiences: any claims for exclusivity can only lead into the same delusion and pretension through which Europe of the nineteenth century believed itself to represent the rest of the world, and entitled to dominate it. Its borders can only be those it runs up against in the course of its own internal civilizing process. And even at those boundaries it ought not to react hyper-sensitively but rather – and for the first time in its history – as a sensible Whole.

This project need not be limited to quiet pathos. Why should Europeans indulge any less in the joy of their diversity than the Swiss? A European federation is not merely a novelty of human history; the fact that it has never existed before is a source of inspiration more than of caution and circumspection.

In its organization Europe must be as resourceful as life itself, which modern bioscience no longer sees as a goal-oriented process, as a natural counterpart to divine history, but rather as a patchwork, an ongoing search for equilibrium in unstable niches: a kind of ongoing game of questions and responses addressed to a 'globalized' environment that is both threatening and sustaining. Thus, all European organs, head and limbs, 'Brussels' and the old nation-states, become bearers of a process of intelligent self-creation. This Europe does not fear for its identity for the simple reason that it is conceivable only as a product of political ecology, and has no need for the (always idle) propaganda of identity. Europe may content itself with the fact of its civil existence: a historical first-class novelty as well.

To put it melodramatically: Europe shares a common destiny. The Stoic school of ancient Greece described the concept of *Amor Fati*, the 'love of fate'; it was never convenient, but it was by no means passive. In order to build Europe, one does not have to love it. But one may.

Neue Zürcher Zeitung

---

[1] The *acquis communautaire* refers to the complete body of European Union treaties, laws, regulations, and directives, including rulings by the European Court of Justice. Absent a future European Constitution, the *acquis communautaire* constitutes the settled law of the Union; its acceptance is the basic condition for entry for potential EU members.

THE EUROPEAN UNION FACES THE MAJOR POINTS OF ITS DEVELOPMENT

Gianni Vattimo

The program that characterized Romano Prodi's mandate as President of the European Commission can be considered achieved.

The Union has come to include ten new countries. Thus, the long-delayed need to draw up a constitution and devise a more adequate structure than the multilateral treaties that have marked the Union's development in the past decades has become ever more urgent. The process has entered its conclusive phase (the only missing step is that of obtaining ratification from the parliaments or popular referenda of the various countries). However, a risk has now emerged, which after all was to be expected: that a widened European Union might mean a 'diluted' Union. In order to stay together with no frictions or contrasts, these countries, so numerous and in many aspects so different from each other, seem to be in need of a structure able to provide extreme autonomy, an autonomy that might undermine precisely the more explicit federal bond which is the goal of the new European Constitution.

This explains the palpable ambiguity in the statements of many individuals of all political stances who express their enthusiasm for the new possibilities afforded to the Union. Some regard its enlargement – as was Prodi's goal – as a decisive incentive for a less vague unity of Europe, one that will make it an acknowledged and influential participant in world politics. Others hope that the increase from fifteen to twenty-five member countries will force the Union to greatly limit its 'federal' ambitions and continue to rely instead, for many more years, on the so-called 'intergovernmental method.' This method requires unanimity for every crucial decision (defense, taxes, foreign policy, justice…), and has so far been adopted for most of the major political issues.

From the point of view of these limitations, the federal future of Europe – a condition unanimously considered indispensable in order for Europe to have an influential presence on the world scene – appears to be rather desperate. Perhaps, however, it is not so, since in the very treaties that have governed the institutions of the Community so far there is mention of an instrument that can be adopted as long as it is politically desired, one usually indicated with the expression 'two-speed Europe.' Sometimes this expression meets shocked reactions, because it seems to establish unacceptable differences (between first-class and second-class countries). Nevertheless, this instrument has often been employed with good results, starting with the adoption of a common currency. As is well known, only some of the countries that form the Union also share the euro as their currency, while giants such as Great Britain maintain their own currency. And yet, the euro somehow works, and at any rate, if it is less successful than one would like, that has nothing to do with Great Britain's absence, but, if anything, with the fact that it is not yet backed up by an actual federal economic policy. The two-speed method could – and in our opinion should – be adopted also, and especially, in order to implement tighter federal structures, beginning with foreign policy, defense, and the economy. Of course, this should merely constitute an anticipation of ties meant to include more and more member countries which, thanks to the experimentation carried out by this initial group, might find valid reasons to join it.

But is there a European identity? On this point we run up against the limits of our historical experience. We are in fact born out of a history of national states that were conceived –

not always in a 'realistic' manner, but in any case in the generally shared social rhetoric – as homelands founded by 'arms,
language, faith,' etc., and as such legitimized, in their will for
unity and independence, by 'natural' motives. A similar
'national' consciousness with regard to Europe is unthinkable.
Indeed, what we find fascinating when we consider the plan
of a politically unified Europe is precisely the almost complete
absence of 'natural' bases connected to any national consciousness. Europe can only exist as a unity of 'cultures' also and
above all in contrast to 'nature.' Even if we don't see natural,
'organic' elements of cultural belonging such as language, race,
soil, and religion that would make us feel European – in fact,
we would consider them mistakes, a sort of regression to the
nineteenth century of nationalities – we must recognize and
try to articulate explicitly the reasons why, especially in recent
times, we realize nonetheless that being European makes a
difference, a difference that comes before and that is more
fundamental than our belonging to that work-in-progress
which is the European Union.

It is by articulating that difference that we can perhaps discover
our European identity, without which the unquestionable pragmatic reasons that prompt us to build a federal Europe would
seem too unpersuasive to promote any shared political commitment from anyone except those 'appointed for the job.' These
pragmatic reasons are of course undeniable, starting from the
one which animated the founders of the first European
Community, that of coal and steel, the ECSC. First the ECSC,
then the European Common Market, and finally the euro helped
to put an end to wars among the countries in the continent,
and to make Europe richer and more competitive.

However, pragmatic reasons of interest are not enough. The
interests that must be reconciled by politics are often in radical
contrast to each other, to the point that, in order to reach an
agreement, a sort of 'enlarged mentality ' is needed, that is, an
ethical decision that won't limit itself to reckoning what would
be more profitable to each in terms of economic gain or even

in terms of general welfare. Are we, then, searching for something analogous to the patriotic values that during and before the nineteenth century served to build national states and ensure their independence? Yes and no: we are not searching for naturalistic or organic values, values of 'original' belonging. And yet, we are looking for something that could assert itself from the point of view of functional rationality, as well as motivate an ethical–political choice, not only one of more or less immediate profit. In many ways, we can discover these essentially paramount values by examining the reasons that make us feel European in spite of all the natural differences that separate us. Europe vs. the United States. On this point we cannot but make reference to what we recently experienced on the eve of the Anglo-American invasion of Iraq, when Rumsfeld claimed that there is an old Europe which can be ruled out of the game because it is unable to keep up with the times, and that the new Europe coincides instead with the countries willing to participate in the coalition made up of the United States' 'willing' collaborators. Rumsfeld's speech filled us with indignation, and not only for reasons of primogeniture – since that 'old' Europe included some of the countries that contributed most to the birth of the very notion of the European Union (and Great Britain, Spain, or Poland were certainly not among them).

Frankly speaking, what made us indignant was above all the fact that it was the representatives of the Bush administration who seemed to be making decisions regarding Europe; and that, by excluding France, Germany, and the Italy of De Gasperi and Spinelli, these representatives really seemed to betray the European spirit, in the way we are accustomed to understand it. That which Rumsfeld and Bush call Europe is characterized by values that we do not perceive as our own; and therefore, by contrast, it evokes in us the awareness of what Europe 'truly' is.

First of all – even though the list could be drawn up in a different order according to each individual as well as 'national' sensibility – there is a radical difference in terms of secularism. We are certainly familiar with the religious roots of North American society; we know about the deep influence of the Pilgrim Fathers and their search for an absolute, religiously inspired freedom of conscience. But in the version provided by Bush and his friends, the profound, 'libertarian' religiosity that characterizes the American spirit has ended up manifesting itself as what we fear it really is: the notion that 'God is with us,' and that the proof of it is our economic and military superiority.

The different, and perhaps more tormented, secularism of Europe reveals a different perception of the State and its function. We could simplify all of this by declaring that Europe's DNA contains a gene of 'socialism' completely unknown to the United States. There are deeply historical reasons for this difference: in the United States, the centrality of local, state, and federal governments came 'after' forms of 'pioneer' self-organization. The institution of the State in the United States is, on its various levels, 'tolerated' rather than regarded as an active factor of social life.

From education to health care to the business world, the prevailing position of American society is to leave matters to private individuals and their self-organization. Ultimately, this extremely 'laissez-faire' view of institutions might find its roots in the abundance of physical space that Americans have enjoyed so far.

The Europe we live in, so rich in history and poorer and poorer when it comes to empty spaces, cannot conceive of the State as merely a subsidiary form. Even the most libertarian among us realize that the space for free competition cannot be safeguarded without a strong regulatory presence of public institutions. And this is the gene of 'socialism' which, despite every misfortune encountered by actual socialism, still survives in European culture.

As a logical consequence, in European societies (in the republics that emerged after ousting monarchies, for example) social competition is, from the very beginning and not only in a subsidiary or 'supplementary' manner, regulated by public institutions. Granted, this might account for the European bad habit of always expecting everything, or in any case too much, from government. But it also provides a less harshly Darwinian concept of social life. In a way, it can be regarded as a much 'slower' notion of 'development,' of a development which even in the United States has started to reveal itself as an overly quantitative ideal, one which cannot but have a negative effect on the quest for individual happiness, despite the fact that the latter is an acknowledged right.

As we continue to reflect upon why we feel European and not American, we are bound to encounter a different view of existence, a different notion of what constitutes a 'good life,' a different existential plan. And we are also bound to encounter a vision of participatory democracy that excludes the rigid hierarchies that originate (almost) necessarily in societies where natural differences, rather than being corrected by the State, are cultivated and utilized for the 'development' of the system.

It is for reasons logically tied to the ones here enunciated only roughly but widely felt in the consciousness of all Europeans that, as Croce would say, 'we cannot help but call ourselves Europeans,' also and above all to the extent that our spirit differs from the currently prevailing spirit in American society. And our hope is that this difference will become the inspiring principle for a political system able to bestow on Europe the dignity and significance it deserves in world politics.

La Stampa

HUMILIATION OR SOLIDARITY?

Richard Rorty

President Bush's National Security Advisor has said, according to American newspapers, that Russia will be forgiven, Germany ignored, and France punished. Whether or not Condoleezza Rice actually used those words, they express the attitude of the Bush administration toward nations that failed to join the Iraq war coalition. Disagreement with Washington by foreign governments is being treated by the Bush White House not as honest difference of opinion, but as the failure of knaves and fools to accept guidance from the wise, farsighted, and benevolent.

Rice herself (the former provost of my university) is a very sophisticated and knowledgeable person, and so it is unlikely that she thinks of European leaders in any such simplistic way. But her views on the imperative need for America to retain total control of international affairs are consonant with the remark that the American press is now attributing to her. Presumably she thinks that people like Joschka Fischer and Dominique de Villepin, though neither fools nor knaves, must nevertheless be publicly humiliated, in order to help ensure a stable world order. For such stability will be possible only if America's hegemony goes unchallenged.

More frightening than the bullying tone adopted by President Bush's advisors is the fact that European heads of government and foreign ministers are reverting to their bad old habits. They are competing with one another for Washington's favor. After so many decades of dependence, it is very hard for Europe's leaders to stop judging their success in foreign affairs by the extent to which they are on cordial terms with the great imperial power. But just in so far as they continue to do this, it will be easy for Washington to set them against one another – to make them behave like schoolchildren vying for the teacher's favor.

Jürgen Habermas and Jacques Derrida argue that 'At the international level and in the framework of the UN, Europe has to throw its weight on the scales to counterbalance the hegemonic unilateralism of the United States.' If the statesmen of '*Kerneuropa*' ('core Europe') adopt the stance that Habermas and Derrida recommend, and act in concert to assert their independence of Washington, the US government will do everything possible to turn American public opinion against them. Refusal to accept the American magisterium will be viewed by most of the American media as a sign of moral weakness. Washington will also do its best to set the members of the EU against one another, in order to ensure that *Kerneuropa*'s audacity does not become an example for the EU as a whole. For the last thing Washington wants is a Europe that is sufficiently united and self-confident to question America's hegemony. If the citizens and governments of *Kerneuropa* act as Habermas and Derrida hope they will, Washington will use every trick in the book to get them back in line – willing, as in the past, to let their country's votes in the UN be determined by the decisions made by Rice and her colleagues on the National Security Council. For Bush's advisors suspect that if the EU had held together – if its member governments had been unanimous and vociferous in their repudiation of Bush's adventurism – they would never have been able to persuade the American public to agree to the war in Iraq.

Yet if the citizenry and the governments of Europe do not seize the hour, if they do not carry through on the repudiation of American unilateralism manifested on February 15, then Europe is unlikely ever again to play a significant role in determining the future of the world. The leaders of France, Germany, Benelux, Italy, and Spain cannot postpone the choice they have to make: whether to accept the humiliating subservience that Washington hopes to impose on them, or to break free by formulating and pursuing foreign policy initiatives to which Washington will react with incredulous outrage.

For Americans who were horrified by the willingness of their fellow-citizens (and of the Democratic Party) to support Bush's Iraq war, the acquiescence of European statesmen in American unilateralism would be a tragedy. For if Washington does force Germany to beg not to be ignored, and France to plead for relief from punishment, then the next time an American president decides to embark on an exciting military adventure there will be no significant countervailing pressure from abroad. Remembering what happened the last time that Washington's will was defied, European governments will be loath to instruct their representatives at the UN to question the latest American initiative.

The Bush administration's view that a permanent *pax Americana*, one whose terms are dictated by Washington alone, is the world's only hope has as a corollary that the US must never permit its military power to be challenged. That claim is made explicit in a policy statement titled 'The National Security Strategy of the United States,' which asserts that 'our forces will be strong enough to dissuade potential adversaries from pursuing a military build-up in hopes of surpassing, or equaling, the power of the United States.'

It is possible that even Democratic presidents will, in the future, reiterate this claim to permanent hegemony. The bullying tone adopted by the Bush administration may be one that all future American presidential candidates feel compelled to adopt in order to show themselves 'strong' and 'resolute' in 'making war against terrorism' (an expression that will, from now on, be invoked to excuse anything the American government may choose to do). This may be the case even though

men like Senator Kerry and Governor Dean (the most plausible candidates for the Democratic presidential nomination next
year) understand, as President Bush does not, that no empire
lasts for ever. They are farsighted enough to know that
American economic and military dominance is bound to be
transitory, and to suspect that insistence on perpetual military
supremacy will, sooner or later, produce a confrontation with
China, Russia, or both – a confrontation which may end in
nuclear war. But this knowledge may not suffice to make them
change the direction of American foreign policy.

This means that the European Union is the only likely
sponsor of an alternative to Washington's project of a permanent *pax Americana*. The leaders of the still-fragile regimes that
govern Russia and China are too preoccupied with their own
hold on power, and with domestic problems, to ask themselves
questions about the best course for the world as a whole. Their
resentment at Washington's arrogance will remain tacit. They
can afford to wait for their own day to come – the day on
which they tell Washington that they can and will challenge
its military power. If America refuses to recognize that that day
will come sooner or later, and if Europe does nothing to offer
an alternative scheme for world order, then nothing is likely
to change. Sooner or later we shall recreate the situation that
prevailed during the Cold War – nuclear powers daring each
other to be the first to launch their missiles.

The rulers of at least a dozen countries will soon have their
fingers on nuclear triggers. To believe that Washington can
forever hold all these rulers in awe would be folly, yet it is a
folly that seems likely to prevail. 'The National Security Strategy
of the United States' makes no reference to eventual nuclear
disarmament, but only to nonproliferation. 'Nonproliferation'
means that only regimes that acknowledge American hegemony have the right to possess nuclear weapons. The National
Security document pretends that the danger of nuclear
confrontation ended when the Cold War ended, and takes for
granted that American and Russian submarines, each of them

armed with enough warheads to destroy ten great cities, will lurk beneath the oceans for generations to come.

Prior to the Bush administration, American statesmen usually paid lip service, at least, to the idea that the *pax Americana* was a transition to something better. Most of them realized that American hegemony was a makeshift that would have to do until something more enduring became possible – something like a veto-free United Nations functioning as a global parliament, equipped with a permanent peace-keeping military force, and able to carry out a program of global disarmament. (I once heard a former Republican Secretary of State say, in private, that he would be willing to trade a considerable measure of American national sovereignty for nuclear disarmament.) For Bush and his advisors, however, talk of such a rebuilt UN is pointlessly idealistic, a refusal to face up to reality, a romantic retreat into a dream world.

If any projects for a new international order put forward by the EU are to be of use, they will have to embody the idealism that America has seemingly become unable to sustain. The European Union will have to put forward a vision of the world's future to which Washington will react with scornful mockery. It will have to offer proposals for rewriting the Charter of the United Nations and for putting the UN in charge of a program of global nuclear disarmament. It will have to dream dreams that will strike *Realpolitiker* as absurd. But, as Habermas and Derrida point out, some of Europe's recent dreams have come true. They are right to say that Europe has, in the second half of the twentieth century, found a solution to the problem of how to transcend the nation-state. The European Union – just as it stands, even prior to the adoption of a constitution – is already the realization of what the *Realpolitiker* thought was an idle fantasy. If the sense of shared European citizenship becomes entrenched in the first quarter of the twenty-first century in the way in which the sense of shared American citizenship became entrenched in the first quarter of the eighteenth century, the world will be well on the way to a global confederation. Such a confederation has been recognized, ever since Hiroshima, as the only possible long-term solution to the problem created by nuclear weapons.

'Why shouldn't [Europe] issue a further challenge,' Habermas and Derrida ask, 'to defend and promote a cosmopolitan order on the basis of international law, against competing visions?' Why not indeed? It might just save the world, something that American policy cannot do. At best, America's 'national security strategy' can only postpone disaster. It can only keep things going for another generation or two. If there is ever going to be a time when public opinion must force politicians to be more idealistic than they feel comfortable being, this is it. For all the reasons Habermas and Derrida give, the citizens of core Europe are in the best position to exert such pressure.

If February 15 comes to be seen, as Habermas and Derrida hope it may, as the 'the birth of a European public sphere,' the beginning of a new sense of shared European identity, that would change everyone's sense of what is politically possible. Such an upsurge of idealistic self-redefinition would be responded to around the world, in the US and China as well as in Brazil and Russia. It would break the logjam that we are now trapped in. It is, as far as I can see, about the only thing that might.

Bush's apologists in the American media are likely to dismiss Habermas and Derrida's appeal as just another example of the envious and resentful anti-Americanism that is recurrent among European intellectuals. Such a charge would be completely baseless. Both men have profited from their frequent and extended visits to the US to gain a deep and thorough understanding of America's political and cultural achievements. They are well aware of America's world-historical role as the first of the great constitutional democracies, and also of what America has done for Europe in the years since the Second World War. They appreciate that it was idealistic Wilsonian internationalism in the United States that led to the creation of the United

Nations. They know that the unilateralist arrogance of the Bush administration is a contingent misfortune – neither inevitable nor expressive of something deeply embedded, and irre-deemable, in American culture and society.

Both Europe and America contain many millions of people who see clearly that, despite all that America has done for the cause of human freedom, its assertion of a right to permanent hegemony is a terrible mistake. Americans who realize this need all the help they can get to persuade their fellow-citizens that Bush has been taking their country down the wrong path. The solidification of the European Union into a powerful inde-pendent force in world affairs would be viewed by that segment of American opinion not as an expression of resentful anti-Americanism, but as an entirely appropriate and altogether welcome reaction to the danger that the direction of American foreign policy poses for the world.

Süddeutsche Zeitung

EUROPE, BOTH NEEDED AND IN NEED

Fernando Savater

One of the greatest tragedies of human life, on an individual as well as on a collective scale, is the fact that the resolution to make amends comes only after a disaster has occurred rather than as a result of a serene and rational reflection on what may really be most practical for well-considered self-interest. In one of Jules Verne's first (and best) rite-of-passage novels, *A Journey to the Center of the Earth*, the mentor announces to the young protagonist that he is about to receive a 'lesson in abysses.' It appears that those lessons in abysses are the only means through which one's conduct can be regenerated; they are also the most effective way for nations to change their erratic or depredating course and search for shared solutions to their problems. Undoubtedly, one of the most recent and significant 'lessons in abysses' we have received – the consequences of which are still cropping up – is the punitive war against Iraq.

This massive aggression against a dictatorship that not so long ago still enjoyed such acquiescence on the part of our democracies (and even of the countries that have attacked it) has convincingly shown the impotence of international law. It has also cleared the path – a path we are unfortunately rushing through at an increasingly fast pace – to a world order based exclusively on the hegemonic will of the greatest military power, and not on agreements reached jointly by countries under the rule of law. The fragile international institutions forged in the past century appear to have been abolished or, at least, relegated to a museum of good political intentions which are no longer legitimate in today's harsh and conflicted world scenario. In the face of this return to nothingness, and after this 'lesson in abysses,' the European countries aspiring to be effectively united – and today they are further from such unity than ever – must consider a change in historical direction.

Of course, none of the large European states can credibly seek to reprimand or reproach the United States for its imperial pretensions. Our European bellicose and colonialist tradition makes us inappropriate judges of ambitions which, until recently, have been our own, and which we may even have invented. However, the two tragic world wars that broke out in our continent have convinced most Europeans that it is essential to search for internationally regulated formulas to prevent, avoid, and solve, as a last resort, confrontations between opposing interests, on a scale beyond nation-state boundaries. The goal must certainly be to administer the world's material resources, such as oil, energy or water, but it also ought to be to protect social values such as education, democratic liberties, and human rights. Security is, without a doubt, an important principle. However, today it has become evident that the world will become more secure if the efforts are geared to fight, not only terrorism, but poverty, inequality, and injustice, both political and economic. More than six billion human beings cannot continue to live in hostile tribes ruled by intransigent deities, without the establishment of the rule of law, and without offering any real support to the world's weakest members. What is important is not only to be in the right and defend one's position or impose it with arms, but to apply the force of social development in order to establish the principles of a universal reason in which all human beings can regard themselves both as accomplices and beneficiaries. The idea of progress, which was born and several times corrupted in Europe, ought to go beyond a superficial 'modernization' geared to overcome obstacles for the deployment of capitalism. It should refer, instead, to a struggle to promulgate rights and duties that respect humanity as a plural creation. 'Civilization' must be understood as something more than the mere 'modernization' of markets and technology.

Although it may not be sufficient, Europe's role is indispensable for such a civilizing project. That Europe must be united not merely in terms of the cosmopolitan ideals of the Enlightenment but in order to safeguard subsequent conquests, such as the welfare state, a secular sense of the political order, and civil rights for all (a long time ago the French philosopher Jean-Pierre Faye pronounced the eloquent motto: 'Europe is where there is no death penalty'). This European unity needs a constitution that establishes those fundamental principles institutionally. It also needs a common voice in foreign policy and a dissuasive military capacity to guarantee the continent security without having to resort to the interested protection of other powers. This is not to call for a European Union that is a closed fortress but to advocate a Europe so strongly coherent as to remain open and passionately generous to the global needs that can be denied to no human being. Today, more than ever, our nations need the rest of the world because terrible threats have shown us that not even the most powerful nations can live in isolation. Nonetheless, it is also true that the world needs that European voice, harmonic and clear in its characteristic pluralism. It is time for European citizens, both the 'progressive' and the 'civilized' – in the most responsible sense of the word – to demand that our governments take the measures needed to make that united effort effective. This will enable us to prove, at least, that we have advantageously learned those lessons in imminent abysses.

El País

2

INITIAL RESPONSES

THE END OF EUROPE

Barbara Spinelli

It is still unclear what Giscard had in mind when, after being nominated Chairman of the Convention entrusted with drawing up a constitution for Europe, he announced that the task of the continent was of historical proportions. It was not very different from the task assigned to the members of the Philadelphia Convention, he said, and it, too, was to pave the way for a federal constitution like the one drawn up in the United States in 1787. Apparently, then, the French ex-chief of state intended to achieve something grandiose: a Europe capable of action and not only talk; a Europe willing to reunite with its own Orient after half a century of separation but unwilling to be limited by the right to veto, a right which each country can exercise in a Union that by now includes twenty-five member-states. Instead, the right to veto is maintained intact in the very fields where Europe needs to grow and develop the most, that is, in foreign policy and defense in Giscard's proposal, inscribed in the constitution draft he presented to the Convention members and to the member-states. In the now larger Union no decision regarding these matters can be made if all of the states have not reached a previous agreement. Now, this is a way to diminish the import-ance of our continent to the point of rendering it totally irrelevant, and on this issue intellectuals were right to express their preoccupation with Europe's decline in articles published in various European newspapers. The initiative stemmed from

Habermas and Derrida, who were followed, among others, by Gianni Vattimo in this same newspaper, Umberto Eco in *La Repubblica*, and Fernando Savater in *El País*. Some of them speak indulgently of a necessary compromise between the Convention and the governments.

Giscard himself suggests that the member-states will otherwise refuse to give their consent when the time comes to adopt the constitution in the intergovernmental conference to be held in October 2003. However, Giscard himself has only focused on the conservative spirit of the nation-states, which for the most part demanded to keep the right to veto, and has ignored the will of the Convention members, who were largely in favor of a different position.

As Tommaso Padoa-Schioppa[1] wrote in the *Corriere della Sera*, Giscard and the Commission 'did not leave room for the individuals in the Assembly to express themselves, and instead took advantage of their drive towards Europe. Thus, they fell prey to their desire to please the European Council and therefore the governments.' In reality, they fell prey to the most detrimental aspects of European history, and it is hard to imagine that they were not aware of it. They drew parallels with American history, but at heart they knew the history they were imitating was much closer to home: a history not of rebirth and newfound identity, but an utterly European history of state dissolution. The intellectuals who responded to Habermas's appeal insist on the originality and diversity of the European experience and invite people to treasure the dissent that exists today between a portion of their continent and Washington.

But Europe teaches us that culture and what Habermas calls 'the power of emotions' are not enough to guarantee the Union's capacity to give itself laws and a political structure. What counts are institutions, decision-making processes, and only when the latter function properly can one speak of the foundation of an identity, or, as Eco puts it, of a common feeling. Today our relations with Washington are tense, but

will or Britain are puppets of us — us has european control

tomorrow they might no longer be; the most urgent need is to find a way to work through politics, regardless of the very object of such politics. A free and independent Poland lost both its liberty and its freedom of movement when it first introduced into its constitution the so-called *liberum veto* and began, in 1600 and 1700, to use it in a systematic and ultimately self-destructive manner. The clause made it possible for every deputy to interrupt parliamentary sessions with the words, 'I do not allow it,' in the same way as the representatives of the countries that form the European Union can today. Every negotiation was broken off as soon as a deputy made use of the veto option, and it was this clause that led the country to ruin; Poland became divided and essentially disappeared from the historical scene for over 120 years. Significantly enough, the powers that aspired to control Poland's fate – Russia, Prussia – radically opposed the abolition of that immobilizing veto, a veto so convenient to those who, from outside, wanted to exercise hegemony over the nation.

The *liberum veto* paved the way for what the patriot Thaddeus Kosciusko called *Finis Poloniae*, the end of Polish independence and of the Polish nation. The fact that today Poland takes no position against this clause that threatens to seal analogously the *Finis Europae* is quite unsettling. Poles should be the first to admonish the states of the Union: instead, they keep quiet and appear willing to side with those who fight to safeguard the unanimity principle.

Poland's silence on the *liberum veto* confirms that, at the same time as Europe is winning its post-Cold War battle and is growing geographically, there are internal and external powers that are attempting to cripple it. Sharp disagreements had divided Europe before and during the Iraq war, and in its aftermath Europe threatens to sink because it is denying itself the instrument that would allow it to exist.

Not by chance, the British government cheers, maintaining that the Convention battle has been won. In the same way, the United States leaders are pleased; they have counted on England

and Poland for months in order to rule over a continent they consider – contrary to Umberto Eco's view of Europe as all but marginal – all the more precious the more divided it is. Of course, this plan won't necessarily succeed: the battle is not over yet. The Convention members might rediscover pride in their vision for Europe, and the states themselves might gain more clarity of mind.

Gianfranco Fini,[2] for example, essentially agrees with Prodi even though he considers his criticism of Giscard excessive: the Constitution draft needs to be reviewed – he says – and the right to veto needs to be abolished 'lest Europe become paralyzed.' The intellectuals summoned by Habermas react in the same way. Their appeal to the governments is explicit, and it is worth heeding: the founding states need to decide on a tighter union, in the same way they did for the euro. Governments that are not ready for it can enter at a later time. It is the idea of a two-speed Europe, the core of which will consist of those who want a true union.

However, in this case, too, the *liberum veto* – the method, not the more or less polemical attitude towards the United States – will have to be the distinguishing factor. This, we believe, is the crucial point missing from the appeals made by intellectuals in Europe.

In order to take action, there cannot be unanimous agreement either with regard to the United States, the Middle East, or our shared culture: this is the essential truth we discover when we participate in collective decisions, a truth that Poland experienced directly. Aspiring to absolute unanimity and to a shared cultural feeling is, at worst, a totalitarian utopia. At best, it is a political suicide that creates much more serious dependence. Being able to make decisions even when goals and viewpoints are not unanimous: the art of politics begins from this preliminary notion, a notion that does not aspire to eliminate divisions, but that still holds on to its existence in spite of these divisions. People discuss, share ideas, and then there comes a time to make decisions, to choose among different positions.

Politics can be possible only if the mechanism that leads from word to action truly functions, and Europe needs this simple mechanism. Of course, it needs other things, as well. It needs a vision, an identity, and financial resources in order to translate vision into fact. However, means and resources can be gathered only when it becomes clear that among Europeans a decision can be made even when not all of the states are in agreement. If not, each state will end up preventing the birth of a real sovereignty for the sake of one that has by now become fictitious, one that is individual and national as opposed to the new sovereignty, which is collective and European. France is the state that, together with Great Britain, defends the right to veto most strenuously.

These two governments disagree on the Iraq issue and on relations with Washington, but on the right to veto their positions coincide: even if they are completely illusory, individual national sovereignties are untouchable. This means that the conversion to Europeanism must occur even within the Union's founding group. And, more precisely, in the mind of its founding country. The latter's flaws are no different from those of Great Britain, but its responsibility is considerably greater. Blair's Great Britain is merely a pawn in the United States' strategy, even when it succeeds in resuming negotiations in the Middle East after the Iraq war. France is condemned to isolation and powerlessness, after a purely nationalistic battle fought against Bush's unilateral doctrines.

And yet, German and Italian leaders still wait for France to determine what course to take, because Europe was always made following decisions from Paris. And Britain, too, makes its moves according to Paris's presence or absence: it is by taking advantage of France's shortsightedness that today London can become a model for Eastern Europeans, and defend its vision of a Europe with no political head, with no sword and no common currency.

It is in Paris that the future of Europe will be decided, and this is why its flaws and illusions have such a serious impact.

The Iraq war has diminished France's sovereignty to no less a degree than it did Britain's. Europe represents a way to restore its loss of sovereignty, but it remains to be seen whether the step will be taken or not. The Polish-style *liberum veto* represents instead the most destructive means to make all of us, French and all Europeans alike, disappear from the places where history is decided and made.

La Stampa, June 1, 2003

---

[1] Tommaso Padoa-Schioppa is an economist and member of the executive board of the European Central Bank.

[2] Gianfranco Fini is Italy's deputy prime minister. See the interview with Fini, 'Europa Federazione e non Super-stato' in *Corriere della Sera*, September 7, 2002.

ARE WE REASONABLE?

Jürgen Kaube

Europe: a political structure in search of a concept. At one time it was the conception of a league of peace and the incorporation of Germany. This conception was realized through political treaties, and freedom of travel and trade; in particular, through the will to live in front of rather than behind the Iron Curtain.

Later, when peace within Europe, in the west, north, and south, ceased to be the primary problem, low inflation rates and a growing administration based on European law were added. The result was an entity almost entirely free of ideas or 'vision.' Apart from the European Commission and ministerial conferences, this political union, so-called, remained little more than a topic for official speeches. Has Europe missed something? Wasn't it something of a relief that the European bureaucratic revolution came about in the absence of any ideals; without a genuine people, a genuine constitution or a genuine community? At last it could be said: whatever comes about without war or revolution needs no concept. Where there is no bloody sacrifice to be justified, but only tax burdens and legal thickets, a 'common will' is of secondary importance.

Thoughts on the European 'Identity'

In his plea for a rebirth of Europe Jürgen Habermas appealed to such a common will of Europeans and their 'identity.' The Iraq war, which is supposed to force this reflection, is not on

European soil and is not waged between Europeans. But it has changed Europe by making strongly divergent interests in foreign affairs within the EU obvious. One perceptible point where this becomes particularly clear is how much closer we are to overcoming national-state interests by the idea of 'Europe.'

Habermas follows a doctrine that makes the 'We-feeling' of peoples into a standard for reasonable politics. 'One of us,' say the citizens, and feel themselves to be a part of the whole. Correspondingly, they also say 'none of us' or 'we don't want to live like that' when they describe the boundaries of their unity toward the outside. The enemy is 'one's own question given shape,' as Carl Schmitt once formulated it, for a world in which sharp, ideological contrasts belonged to the norm.

The End of the Bourgeois Era

To put it slightly less poetically: In political terms, people learn the most from whatever they reject most vehemently. By now, however, modern states have at their disposal instructive images of their enemies, though these are defined in distinctly limited terms. For example, what precisely is it that Europeans ought to learn from them with respect to their present problems of daily life, beyond not wanting to live in an authoritarian state shaped by Islamic beliefs? Liberalism, fascism, communism, and the welfare state were produced by the very same political and economic crisis situation conducted under the banner of 'The End of the Bourgeois Era,' 'Mass Society,' 'Industrial Society,' or 'Late Capitalism.'

Now, the most notable difference can be seen in the gap between regions with liberal democracies and those with illiberal ones. On the one hand, the difference is too great to be informative regarding what the European Union wants. On the other hand, it is also too small. Even illiberal regimes join peace-loving world organizations nowadays; even they grant themselves constitutions in which human rights are matter-of-factly provided for, and, unlike totalitarian dictatorships with

Is social or economic integration more valuable? Can one happen w/o the other?

their expansionist ideology, mostly limit themselves to imposing hardships on their own population.

Nation-building, Development, Sovereignty

The vocabularies that states appropriate to describe themselves have become increasingly similar; when one does not peripherally refer to the values which we cherish today, we rely upon those that we cherished just yesterday: formation of nations, development, and sovereignty.

In this situation, Habermas has high hopes for, perhaps all his hope for, an EU shaped by opposition within the Western world. Not the enemy but the alienated friend is now for him 'one's own question given shape.' Europe in contrast to what? Today's United States. Donald Rumsfeld's caricature of the 'old Europe' is turned against the New World itself. Habermas speaks even of an '*avant-garde*' core Europe. How did French and German politics come to deserve this honorary insignia? Because of their willingness to grant the EU 'certain qualities' of state formation and thus to balance the emerging hegemony of the United States.

The attitude of the European population towards the Iraq war, as expressed in the massive demonstrations of February 15, is supposed to be tapped as a sort of legitimating resource for the search for identity. The political idea thus arises not from a waged war but rather from a rejected one. However, Habermas also knows how easily the consensus of the protest march dissolves once more into dissent when discussed.

'Functional Imperatives'

Here, Habermas himself refers to the most important sociopolitical distinction of his social philosophy. According to this, there are on the one hand the 'functional imperatives' of economic, technological, and administrative systems; on the other hand, there is the necessity of a social integration that can only be achieved through democracy. Functional imperatives are to be found empirically in the EU's norm-free economic and administrative 'system integration.' By contrast a socially integrative or an empathetic Europe (so to speak) is supposed to emerge from the common will and the historical experiences of the European citizenry.

Yet – apart from the fact that the construction of a common will presumably must ignore the plethora of motives and the specific need for demarcation of the almost 400 million European citizens – we might ask, a common will for what? Does Habermas know his European fellow-citizens? And do they know each other? For Habermas, the model for a Europe that is run by one will is the nation-state, which is based on the solidarity of its citizens with one another. Europeans, even if they were to live up to this idea, would have to be able to say to a European citizen of another nationality, 'one of us.'

However, if one wants to produce more than mere compassion in a specific situation – say, as to how to approach Africans – and instead to find a foundation for political unity based on feelings of solidarity, then we might indeed wonder how many Finns or Bulgarians – along with their way of life – a Belgian or Irishman knows at all. And if his solidarity with them is supposed to rest solely on the power of their political imagination, and therefore remain non-partisan, then the empirical content of the word 'Europe' might indeed be questioned.

Favoring the state over the market, Habermas offers several sources for a European mentality: the confidence of the Europeans in state limits on free markets, their relative scepticism towards technological progress, their insistence on ideological neutrality – by which he means religious neutrality – in political decisions. The claim that Europeans are sceptical regarding the productivity of the market certainly does not hold true for the European Commission. A scepticism towards technological progress we probably would not want to claim for many Frenchmen, Belgians, and Swedes. Secularization is scarcely more strongly advanced in Poland, Ireland, and Spain than it is in Canada or Australia. Might Habermas, therefore, always be referring to Germany when he speaks of Europe?

And does he always mean the European elite that he expects to be considered as participants in a continental public?

In fact an uncontested and consensus-based interpretation of shared historical experiences is precisely what is not being forged in Europe. Favoring the state over the market can mean quite a number of things in a region that has been haunted by quite a bit of federal government in the past century. Politics as a means for securing liberty – what might Hungary or the Czech Republic say to that? And what might be the attitude of today's Italians toward the sociological meaning of the distinction between politics and economics?

Taming Capitalism

In order to differentiate Europeanness as a mentality opposed to Anglo-Americanism, the picture of Great Britain is not the only thing that would have to be cleansed of all its European traits. Only with a considerable amount of intellectual desire for abstraction would the United States be seen as a 'figure' composed of a religious non-neutrality in politics (proof for this is a publicly praying president!), neo-liberalism, ambitions for hegemony, and the death penalty. To catalogue social justice as an exclusively European idea would be a case of continental self-righteousness. Whether it is socially more just, for example, to keep someone in comfortably provided long-term unemployment, or to employ someone in a low-wage sector, reducing him to the status of low-wage earner, is open to discussion.

Presumably, the choice between these alternatives also does not follow from considerations of justice, as normative political theory would have it, but from the structure of the industrial and service economy of the respective regions. That Europe has been able to deal with the problem of 'taming capitalism' sounds ambiguous enough in times when capitalism has been tamed to zero growth, allowing the economic leeway for socio-political distribution of wealth to diminish.

The European Union is not a suitable object for tangible cultural projections. It offers rather a good example of the sort of changes modern democracy has undergone in previous decades. The opposite of democracy is no longer dictatorship, but Brussels. Countless decisions that are desired partly by an administrative elite, partly by local lobbies, but would never come about at a national level, are introduced via European law into nation-states.

From the euro through to agricultural policy and the equality of women in the public service sector, from fisheries through to antitrust laws to social security reform, Brussels serves as an example of 'requested directives' for which nobody is immediately held responsible on a national level. And it does function. (Though perhaps not for those who understand 'functioning' as a meaningful relationship between politics and happiness, or liberty.) But on this side of those nominal republican values – those intellectual goods of the elite of the early modern city-states and the English landed aristocracy – the EU functions especially as an administrative device that serves to cool down any heated political topics. What it does not do is provide us with meaningful distinctions.

Frankfurter Allgemeine Zeitung, June 3, 2003

FOREIGN POLICY TURNED INSIDE OUT

Harold James

Sometimes it is amusing when things get turned inside out and the wrong way round. Little children, for instance, often put their clothes on the wrong way round. Generally, though, adults don't like to put their underwear over their jackets. So it is quite peculiar when two prominent European intellectuals launch an initiative in which they call for the relaunching of European foreign policy as a domestic policy for the world. In their search for a new world order they have confused domestic- and foreign-policy thinking in a catastrophically muddled way.

On the face of it there is much to be said for a European rethinking of the world. There is a real risk that the United States will be tempted to ignore the rest of the world. There is a need to think about the shape of the European future and how inclusive or exclusive it should be.

Habermas and Derrida are also right to say that the thinking underlying much of the recent debate about Europe has been unclear. In the absence of any good reason for excluding countries such as Russia or Turkey from the process of European integration, many intellectuals and politicians have fallen back on vaguely cultural assertions about difference, with an implicit claim of superiority. This is profoundly blind to history. How are Russia and Turkey unripe for democracy? After all, only thirteen years before the founding of the predecessor of the European Union, the founder members had undergone terrible experiences of dictatorship, collaboration, and compromise.

In addition, the discussion of cultural superiority occurs without (in a very secular Europe) any reference to Europe's Christian or Judaic heritage. The closest modern Europeans get is to refer to the 'Judeo-Christian legacy' or 'Judeo-Christian traditions,' as if Judaism or Christianity were just about lighting menorahs or singing carols next to a Christmas tree. But they will not or cannot say what are the consequences of belief in a monotheistic religion that sets out a natural law that must be obeyed. M. Giscard d'Estaing wanted to include the kind of language associated with a religious heritage in his draft for a European constitution, but never during the discussions of his convention thought of asking what the Vatican thought.

The gradual erosion of the nation-state in post-1945 or post-1958 Europe has disoriented Europeans, who are used to the nation-state, as well as the philosophers who now want to offer an alternative. The philosophers think that traditional foreign policy (which is about the relationship between states, and the preservation of security) is aggressive and bellicose, and that Europeans have a duty because of their problematical history to renounce it. Old-style foreign policy should be replaced by the adoption of a policy aimed at controlling the dangers of world capitalism, which they call world-level domestic policy, addressed to a universal civil society.

Their stance is a fine example of what has become the European problem. Europeans have greatly exaggerated expectations of what it is that politics can achieve, and so they are always and inevitably disappointed when politics and politicians do not live up to these wishes and demands. There are strong utopian, idealized elements that drive many European thinkers to imagine that it is possible by an act of political will to remake society and establish better people.

Practical *Innenpolitik* is of course about something quite different. It is about maintaining law and order, without which societies cannot function. It is also – in the real Europe of today, as in all other industrial societies – about excluding large numbers of people who would like to be immigrants.

Generalizing domestic policy as normally understood to a
world level – making a universal *Innenpolitik* – would be pretty
hard. Law and order? The problem of lawlessness internationally and of collapsed states is one which if it is to be really
solved requires constant military interventions, of precisely the
type that Derrida and Habermas disapprove of so vigorously.
The Europeans themselves have had a hard time dealing with
the legacy of war atrocities and torture in their own societies.
As they should realize, the strongest arguments for the military
action of the United States, the UK and their allies in Iraq rest
on the long-standing inhumanity of the Ba'athist regime, the
gruesome evidence of which is being excavated daily.

Immigration? A world society would change the immigration debate. The world domestic policy obviously would not
be concerned with excluding outsiders (unless anyone is
concerned about the immigration of little green men from
Mars). But would this mean the delegation of discussion of
rights of residence to each small political sub-unit? Would the
problem of citizenship be discussed on a provincial, district,
town, or village level? Would neighbors vote about who could
move into a street? It is difficult to see that as a basis for a more
just and more open society.

The problems with the positive part of the Derrida/
Habermas agenda are even more substantial. What does controlling world capitalism and harnessing the wild beast of
globalization mean, and why should it be desirable? We should
indeed be concerned about reducing global poverty, but that
is exactly what world capitalism is at the moment doing, with
a rapidity that is unprecedented in history. Where there is a
secure legal framework, even in poor (and quite corrupt) countries such as India and China, there is very rapid growth that
is reducing the absolute number of people living in poverty
throughout the world. The academic evidence of the link
between trade opening and growth is overwhelming.

The greatest obstacles to the global mission of poverty reduction come from countries that close off their markets to the

world market. Because Europeans have on the whole not engaged in this kind of exercise of across-the-board protectionism since the Second World War, they have no idea about how destructive (and also how politically damaging) this kind of backlash against capitalism can be.

Because in addition Europeans have had over the past fifty years a great deal of prosperity, they assume that it is good to leave the world precisely as it is, and that any change will be damaging. But this is a very European view: indeed it is in reality the kind of Eurocentrism that Derrida and Habermas claim to be against, and which they believe that Europe should overcome or transcend. It is deeply parochial.

It should not take too much imagination and willingness to investigate other countries and societies and their problems to see evidence of massive failures and substantial threats to stability. Such lessons are indeed more familiar in post-communist countries, in which a utopian vision of containing capitalism produced notoriously perverse results. It is scarcely surprising that many countries in the 'new Europe' are happier with an American vision which includes change and reform, rather than remaining in a comfortable stasis in which the rules of the game are written by frequently very problematical and unrepresentative governments. Remaking the Middle East, in part through the institution of a free-trade area with liberal and open economies, as suggested in the recent proposal of the US government, is also a step forward.

What all these reforms and changes have in common is that they are intrinsically complicated and demand an application of *phronesis*, practical wisdom. The mechanics of a transition to a better economic order, what should be liberalized when and how, are issues that can be solved only in a concrete way, and where appeals to universal debates and universal principles are not a sure or helpful guide.

What would be the consequences of taking seriously the new philosophical appeal to create a new discursive community based on a world protest potential? A Europe that would turn against markets (and prosperity), while most of the world is going in the opposite direction. A Europe that will be poorer. A Europe that will lose part of its population as they migrate to more dynamic and more liberal regions (and above all to the United States, where we are surrounded by highly educated and skilled Europeans fleeing from the restrictions of the old continent). And a Europe that is more marginal in world affairs.

A Europe that thinks of itself as existing because it offers a contrast to the values of the United States will be a Europe that destroys the values on which modern society is based, and instead returns to that 'anti-capitalist longing' (*Sehnsucht*) that did so much damage in the past not only of Europe, but of the world.

Süddeutsche Zeitung, June 3, 2003

EUROPEANS, AMERICANS, AND THE EXCEPTION OF FRANCE

Gianni Riotta

Who is European and who is American? After the transatlantic disputes over the Iraq war, trade, transgenic foods, and even taste, this question has become quite topical. Following the initiative launched by the last philosopher of the Enlightenment, the German Jürgen Habermas, last weekend a group of European intellectuals and American scholar Richard Rorty (as a guest contributor) discussed all of these issues in various newspapers. Writing in *La Stampa*, Gianni Vattimo takes a conservative position (hopefully he won't interpret this in a negative way: I mean conservative in the classical meaning of the term): Americans and Europeans are and will remain different. It is a 'leftist' version of the idea suggested by American essayist Robert Kagan, according to whom Americans are warriors and children of Mars, whereas Europeans are pacifists and children of Venus (just imagine the warrior Churchill and the pacifist Martin Luther King who right now must be rolling in their graves with laughter). In order to get an idea of how fast history is moving, one only need jump to the conclusion of Umberto Eco's essay, which appeared in *La Repubblica*. Eco does not dwell long on utopia and ultimately states: without a common foreign policy and a military defense plan, Europe will end up counting as much as 'Guatemala.' In *La Stampa*, Barbara Spinelli unites theory and politics: plagued by the threat of vetoes, the anemic constitution proposed by French aristocrat Valéry Giscard d'Estaing might seal the 'decline of Europe.' Philosopher Jacques Derrida (with Jürgen Habermas) changes the tone in *Libération*: in order not to fall into the trap of Eurocentrism, we must open up to others, using the light of reason to understand, not to crush. Who is right? The Scriptures come to mind: those who accept losing their identity will find it, those who defend it with drawn sword (or with drawn machine-gun, as happened in the Balkans) will lose it. Today the United States and Europe have different interests but there is no separation of culture; indeed the two sides of the Atlantic cultures are blended, not opposed. Derrida is worshipped (much like Vattimo and Eco) in American universities, but he would have a hard time (much like Vattimo and Eco) in a Nazi skinhead pub in East Berlin or in anti-Semitic neighborhoods of Paris. It is not a question of passports, it is a question of cultures. Those who accept the integration of different traditions grow stronger, those who try to sterilize them fall behind. Without Jewish physicists, Hitler could not have hoped to have the atomic bomb. So many lament the predominance of the English language, but in the United States Spanish is becoming more and more popular, and soon Mandarin will be the number one language used on the Internet. If you ask me what the main strength of the United States over Europe is, I won't answer the military. I will answer the willingness to welcome Russian poet Joseph Brodsky and make him an American, able to write verse in English. It is the carefree passion for Benigni, Gong Li, Tornatore, and Wenders without the stuffiness of the 'cultural exception' so dear to the French. This is the only true return to origins that I would like to see in Europe: the return to hybridism, the desire to experiment with different cultures, learn from others, just as once, as all other European cities had closed their doors to foreign artisans, only Venice opened up to the art of glass-making and for that very reason became its cradle. Enough with safeguarding books, cheeses, privileges; enough with fearing the outside world: the German parliament refused to grant visas to Indian programmers from Bangalore because they could not speak Goethe's language, and now those young people are enriching Silicon Valley. The Europe that brags about its museum-like past is a dead Europe. On the contrary, the Europe that is willing to go back to its past as a meeting point of different cultures will become an interesting continent. You see, those who are born in the United States are American by right, whereas those who are born in Europe rarely obtain full citizenship. I am reminded of what composer Luciano Berio, who recently passed away, once said to me: 'In the United States there is no high or low music, national or foreign music: everything is welcomed with joy, Broadway, jazz, Stockhausen. It is a sense of freedom that I desire for Europe and Italy.' The future of the world belongs neither to caged-in Europeans nor to arrogant Americans: it belongs to people like Berio, who felt at home everywhere he could do his job, the job of being a free man.

Corriere della Sera, June 4, 2003

THE GHOSTS OF
THE CHOCOLATE SUMMIT

Jan Ross

Is this the hour of birth of a European public? Mobilized by Jürgen Habermas, intellectuals took a stand last weekend in half a dozen daily newspapers on the state of affairs on the continent: Habermas himself, with Jacques Derrida, his long-time philosophical adversary, in both the *FAZ* (*Frankfurter Allgemeine Zeitung*), and the Parisian *Libération*; the authors Adolf Muschg and Umberto Eco presented their views in the *Neue Zürcher* and in *La Repubblica*; and the philosophers Gianni Vattimo, Fernando Savater, and Richard Rorty in *La Stampa*, *El País*, and *Süddeutscher Zeitung*, respectively.

The staging was spectacular; the analysis behind it is just as dramatic. After the Iraq war, and in the closing stages of Giscard's constitutional Convention, Europe has presented itself as weak and discordant, pushed to the periphery of the world stage by the powerful, unilateral United States, torn from within between the old German/French core of unity and new American friends such as Great Britain and Poland. Initiating a debate on Europe that is at the same time a European debate – and in the process confirming the presence of a border-crossing, multivocal 'we' through the very process of searching for it – is a masterpiece of political thinking, and one cannot but take off one's hat to Jürgen Habermas's presence of mind, his organizational talent, and his professional ethos as a public intellectual.

But how is this politics of ideas faring? Habermas and his allies propagate a 'core Europe' (there are nuances here, more of that later, but the impulse and the project are common), which means the strengthened collaboration of an *avant-garde* of nations that are willing to unify, especially when it comes to foreign and security policies. This is, to put it in unkind terms, the ideology for the 'chocolate summit': a cranky postwar alliance between France, Germany, Belgium, and Luxembourg. Italy, too, without Berlusconi, could be imagined in this circle, and would be welcome. The current claim that such a European core has no exclusionary tendencies, and no potential for hardening positions between member-states, may be inviting and attractive to the rest of the continent, but is far from convincing. At present, at the very least, 'core Europe' would be nothing other than a declaration of war on the United States as well as on their British or Polish allies; the latent and half-declared division would become manifest and permanent.

'What is European?' So runs the main question of the whole undertaking. The answer seems to read more or less clearly: anything that is not American. Jürgen Habermas collects his elements of a European identity with some care. Secularization, social justice, ecology and scepticism toward new technology, turning away from the law of the jungle, and, when in doubt, somewhat more government than market. With each declaration, the reader says to himself: 'In contrast to George W. Bush.' Habermas knows and says that the fundamental European values are not exclusively European; they are Western and ultimately universal. Furthermore, with Richard Rorty he also has an American on board, a thinker from the left, who is hoping for help from a self-confident, independent Europe for that other, better, and true United States.

The contribution of Umberto Eco, masterful as always, remains entirely free of resentment against the United States. What he fears for Europe, if it fails to merge more tightly, is not so much an external lack of power, but rather an inner decay as it bumbles along. Referring to integrated foreign and security policies, Eco has in mind concrete interventions in those areas of specifically European interest, for which NATO might not always be suited. Thus, Eco too defines European commonalities as comfortably true-to-life and historically saturated both with the memories of the wars of the twentieth century and in the suddenly noticeable feeling of fraternity amongst European tourists or overseas delegates. From this laid-back perspective, the United States is not hostile, not 'the other,' but simply different.

The Learning Difficulties of Eastern Europe

In Habermas's overall program, however, the contrast to the United States provides the main criterion for European self-definition. The Italian philosopher Gianni Vattimo, who is also a member of the EU parliament, clearly identifies his anger with the Bush administration as the driving force behind the search for identity, and utters the malign name, 'Rumsfeld.' In the end, he concludes that Europeans could discover through their confrontation with the United States 'a different vision of existence, a different perception of the "good life," and a different existential project.' The birth of Europe was shaped by a famously malicious remark from Washington.

Habermas, of all people, cannot take comfort in this. But through the mixture that is presented here, these political debates, having emerged partly from conflicts over political principles, are raised to fundamental matters of life, basic questions of existence. This mixture and these dynamics are not unknown historically. They are the developmental dynamic of nationalism. There is apparently a Euro-nationalism, or at least the need for it as catalyzed by the new American forcefulness. One can only wonder where the faith in the harmlessness of such proclamations of pride and uniqueness comes from, where previous European nationalisms have caused such devastation. Is it truly that much different and better, if, instead of the virtues of being German, French, or Italian, the merits of Europeanness are now praised and are supposed to be endowed with such international standing?

With its history of success since the late 1940s in the detox-ification and reconciliation of the previous century, Europe seems in the eyes of many to be above suspicion; whatever serves this project, whatever happens in its name and interest, will be welcome; no warning lights. 'Europe' appears like the last credo bequeathed by the European left after it had to bid farewell to socialism. One can at least appear to be still a bit socialistic, in contrast to the United States where, as everyone knows, raw capitalism rules. And even a little classical belief in enlightenment and progress may have to be revitalized if it opposes George W. Bush's excessive Christian bigotry. 'In our latitudes,' notes Jürgen Habermas, in that most beautiful pride in progressivism, 'a president who begins his daily official duties with public prayer and who combines his political decisions of consequence with a divine mission, is hard to imagine.' Quite true. But this is also a bit cheap and thin, coming as it does from the pen of a philosopher who only recently, in debates over bio-ethics, has found a redeeming social role for religion. In addition, the core European social model does not shine so brightly in the midst of a crisis of the welfare state, compared with America's much-maligned neo-liberalism. Europeanness *à la* Habermas appears curiously on the defensive, if not almost backward, as the guardian of the achievements of Brussels and Bonn, as nostalgia for the good old times before 1989, before globalization, before September 11, and before the eastward expansion of the EU.

As a European event, 1989 does not even rate a mention in this concept; the 'new' Europeans are only disruptive factors. 'The Central and Eastern European countries,' notes a very tight-lipped Jürgen Habermas, 'while certainly working hard for their admission into the EU, are nevertheless not yet ready to place limits on the sovereignty that they have so recently regained.' That we are dealing with more than a transitional phenomenon and a learning deficit, that the Polish or the Baltic peoples perhaps have something worthwhile to say, does not seem to occur to Habermas at all. Adolf Muschg even offers a mild threat from Switzerland: 'And while it may be historically and culturally valid to claim that Europe lives from its contradictions, European politics cannot abide any thoughtless contradictions. It must take care of this threat institutionally. Because what enables the Europeans to work with each other and with themselves is so precious that it must be bearable and must be sustained and preserved in an effective federal body.' There is something crude in this kind of language, and it can only be explained as that overarching moral superiority that Habermas or Muschg ascribe to the Brussels integration project, as if it were the most natural thing in the world. Wherever the post-national Good is dragged in, a few bits of international courtesy will probably be dropped.

Experiences with Tyranny

Yet more than just tactlessness hides in this blindness toward the 'new' Europe. The East of the continent has something to tell the West, and whoever refuses to listen does so at his own peril. In this respect, it is not just opportunism that led the coalition countries in the Iraq dispute to the side of the United States; it's hard to attribute such motives to a man like Václav Havel. The fresh experience of dictatorship makes the struggle against tyrants more compelling. The status quo that core Europeans love so much, and which they now defend against the revolutionary United States, is in the East still connected with the memory of a half-century of oppression. The legacies of 1989 are the primacy of freedom and the hope for something new. A Europe that would deny this legacy will petrify, and finally become desolate.

Die Zeit, June 5, 2003

THE EUROPEAN UNION AND THE UNITED STATES: THE VALUES WE DEFEND

A Response to Riotta

Gianni Vattimo

As expected, thanks to the relevance of the issues that emerged, as well as to the prestige of many of those who intervened (yes, I was among them, but the others were personalities of the caliber of Habermas), the open discussion on Europe that started with the various articles published in several major European newspapers on May 31 has increasingly broadened.

One of those who have joined the discussion is Gianni Riotta (another remarkable personality). In the *Corriere della Sera* of June 4, Riotta briefly summarizes the points of the various contributions (contributions which, after all, are not in contrast to each other). In his article, Riotta stigmatizes a certain 'conservative' tone that can be detected in all contributions, conservative at least in the sense that we agree about reclaiming our European identity, an identity that differs from the American one, and an identity that we should try to maintain, contrary or parallel to American hegemony. According to Riotta, this position is conservative, since in reality, Europe's most unique and fruitful characteristic is the fact that it used to be a meeting point of different cultures. This is what Europe should try and become once again, rather than hardening up in its defense of a rigid identity that threatens to make it impervious to all that is new.

As is evident, Riotta's argument merely reproduces a less coarse version of Rumsfeld's 'old' and 'new' Europe. Riotta is certainly not siding with the Defense Secretary and his group of right-wing Straussians, but only because – and this image really sounds a little retro – he feels and experiences (in New York City, which is not a very American metropolis) the United States the way our fathers and grandfathers did: as the land of tolerance, of wide open spaces, of endless opportunities. In other words, the United States he talks about is the United States we also loved, and in the name of which we defend our 'European' values that we feel are being betrayed by Bush and his administration. Is Admiral Poindexter – the individual who was appointed by Bush to build a 'complete' electronic network meant to monitor the actions of all those who tread on United States soil – a champion of the open, welcoming United States that Riotta is still inspired by? Riotta will answer that, precisely in order to help the 'true' United States not to be swept away by the reactionary wave that has formed there after September 11, one must not overestimate the influence of those who rule it today and who promote Bush's politics throughout the world. However, it is just as sensible, if not more sensible, not to trust in the illusion that Europe will be able to help the United States mend these tendencies by operating from within an unquestioned (and old) Atlantic bloc.

This has been Blair's strategy and so far, if only judging from the scanty approval it has received from the British people, it hasn't been very successful.

La Stampa, June 6, 2003

HOW BIG IS
THE EUROPEAN DWARF?

Péter Esterházy

Once, I was an Eastern European; then I was promoted to the rank of Central European. Those were great times (even if not necessarily for me personally), there were Central European dreams, visions, and images of the future; in short, everything (everything one needs for a round table, but that is spoken in haste and unfairly). Then a few months ago, I became a New European. But before I had the chance to get used to this status – even before I could have refused it – I have now become a non-core European. It's like someone who has always lived in Munkács, and has never left Munkács in his entire life, but who has been, nevertheless, a one-time Hungarian, one-time Czech, one-time citizen of the Soviet Union, then a citizen of the Ukraine. In our town, this is how we become cosmopolitans.

Europe must shape up, they say. 'Core Europe' to the fore, Jürgen Habermas has demanded recently. Europe is dissenting, however.

I am in Budapest, sitting in a room far away from the discussion of this issue. Around here, you can hardly hear this discussion, even though it seems practically all the best and brightest are speaking out on the subject. Perhaps it needn't be so (there is the Internet here, and four or five German-speaking television channels, etc.), but that's just the way it is. But it's not just that the discussion remains remote from Budapest: Budapest itself is far away from the discussion. 'Beginning in core Europe' – to put it in a slightly exaggerated form – is nearly the only aspect of Habermas's train of thought that's coming through to us. And while I see no serious reason for not translating this new division (core/non-core) with the terms 'first-class' and 'second-class,' still, I'd rather not speak in that habitual Eastern European, forever insulted way.

I can well understand Habermas's automatic response; his 'beginning' is quite logical, at the beginning. Seeing the new EU member-states as a disruptive factor is nothing more than a rational, sober observation (or feeling). It is and will remain difficult to act in concert with the newcomers. Although we newcomers like to point out that we, too, have always been Europeans, we still march to a different tempo, so to speak. For us, things are important that might not be important for others; we are aware of different things, and we use words differently. For example, by freedom we understand not, as you might think, the balance of rights and obligations, but the chance for survival, the inventive concealment from authority, continuous muddling-through. And during the time of the dictatorship we learned that the State is an enemy that must be deceived at every opportunity. And yet we also expect it to solve all our problems. We've just recently regained our sovereignty, but we have not yet figured out what it is all about, and already we have to put limits on it again.

In our eyes, the United States has never been the great power; it has always been a dream. An important dream: the shining knight on the white horse who rides in to carry us away. Of course nothing like this ever happened (think of 1956). Yet this dream remains fundamentally unaltered. For our part, we couldn't experience the arrogance of this great power directly – nor the heavy burden of the help we had received. There was no 1968 here; there was no student movement and no reappraisal of the past. In a dictatorship there is nothing but the dictator. And people.

And Derrida Has No Time

Or let's just have a look at current events. February 15, 2003 saw huge demonstrations everywhere in Europe. We had them here, too: about thirty people were involved, and they promptly began arguing over party loyalties. We watched the demonstrations on television. Social passivity like this is also a product of the experience of dictatorship. How else could we explain the fact that the so-called conservative parties (also right-wing extremists) opposed the war, while the socialists supported it? Or better, both sides preferred not to decide at all. This sentiment, 'if nothing happens, there won't be any trouble,' is also a reaction to the Kádár period. Now, however, we have trouble. The driving force for that letter of the eight countries was less loyalty towards Bush than powerlessness, a lack of diplomatic experience, and political clumsiness. Yet, how can someone suddenly become adept from one moment to the next; what tradition is this diplomatic skill supposed to arise from? What kind of support would one have?

It is really as the poet says: Central Europe can only be understood from the vantage point of Central Europe; and to be a Central European means to not know oneself.

So there is this Other. With this Other hardly anything has happened since 1989; we haven't handled our own problems; no one could do anything with us. Since the East had broken into the West with the GDR, one could hope for a moment that Germany would take note of it and would want to get to know this Other (know itself, so to speak). But that's not the way it was. (And people try to compensate for it in the most disparate ways.)

Now we have the new, ever-changing world order on our backs, a strong United States, a confused Europe, changing so fast that even Derrida had no time to write his own article. One had to act, and to do so as quickly as possible, and this is really most easily accomplished with an advance party. Enlightened absolutism has been able to solve problems of this

kind (apart from dictatorships) most effectively. This 'beginning' is an expression that could have come from Catherine
the Great.

Now, we're offered this Core Europe as the locomotive of
the *avant-garde*; the doors of this train are open, out of self-
interest, and we can (in our own interest) jump aboard. It's a
wonderful image, not even all that oversimplified. But I find
it problematic only because the tracks are so newly laid. It is
true that East–Central Europe is a disruptive factor, but if we
only see such a factor in it, what do we want to talk about?
And while it's not in my interest to pose the following question, I'll do it anyhow: What is this EU expansion for? Out of
altruism, out of courtesy?

That is too little, that is nothing. But we cannot avoid
ourselves. Eastern Europe must learn to behave like an adult,
like someone who can make real decisions with real consequences; and that means responsibility. Western Europe, on the
other hand, cannot avoid getting acquainted with the disruptive factors, which cannot be taken care of with mere gestures.
(Or with the lack of such gestures; think of the matter-of-fact
arrogance of the French president as he observed that the new
countries had failed to make use of the possibility of silence.
Bon. For me, French arrogance is the kind that I love best in
the entire world. If one is to have arrogance, then, at least let
it be French; this is stylistically the greatest thing which the
European mind is able to produce; Hungarian arrogance is
ridiculous, *voilà*, the German form is ponderous, the Italian
one too loud; perhaps the English form is all right, too, but it
is so refined that it remains very quiet.)

Helplessness is in Vain

Seen from here, from the moon, the feelings of resentment
towards the United States in the newly formulated definition
of Europe appear shortsighted, much more like a tactical
maneuver. In my opinion, such feelings can be neither a starting
point nor a goal, much like efforts toward a desirable balance

between the United States and Europe. Something like this can only be a result. In my opinion, a common interest can scarcely be made a subject of discussion. It is more likely that it would become visible in the context of individual movements, reactions, and by a significant proportion of those involved. And it is as if the United States were concealed by Bush. The United States is, in my opinion, just like us, only different. But it is no second pole which we could use to determine our own position. To put it politely, we will not fare very well with such sophomoric sentiments as 'May the better man win.' And once again: what are we really talking about?

In the competition of new ideas about the new European self-consciousness, I have the odd feeling that we wanted a new giant national state, feelings of identity, a common enemy, and, instead of national character traits, Euro-national character traits. (An old joke reads like this: 'How big is the Soviet dwarf? Gigantic!') A structure such as the United States of Europe does not appear desirable either. Compared with the United States, the differences between us are simply too great. The distance between Hamburg and Kiel is greater than that between Boston and San Francisco. But then, I haven't even gotten as far as Hódmezövásárhely yet.

Up to now, Europe has been united, spiritually, by dictatorships. By resistance to dictatorships. But what has been happening since 1989? Where are the training grounds for developing an organic thinking, one that could generate an image of Europe? They don't exist. Besides, we are afraid, and rightly so, afraid of visions. If I were of a more apocalyptic disposition, I would describe Europe and the spirit of Europe as a corpse, and then what we would experience as a culture would be the posthumous growth of our fingernails. Yet, shocked at my vision, I withdraw it forthwith (and if I should forget to withdraw it, I will surely do so on my death bed).

Habermas writes that 'an attractive, even infectious vision does not fall from the sky. Today, it can only be born from a disturbing sense of helplessness.' These are important sentences.

But it's as if this general helplessness were not disturbing at all; in fact it seems to be quite calm. Calm helplessness is a void. Starting from there we can only arrive at the tired equation, EU = the euro + Brussels.

The first step would be to become restless. One would then have to find a common disquieting element (take note of this!).

Süddeutsche Zeitung, June 11, 2003
Translated by Judith Sollosy

Action out to
self - interest or
evangelizing
missions ?

THE VIEW FROM UP TOP:

Core Europe from the Scandinavian Perspective

Aldo Keel

In the course of the debate over a multi-speed Europe recently touched off by Jürgen Habermas, many have expressed a desire for common foreign, security, and defense policies for 'core Europe' as a counterbalance to the unilateralism of the United States. Is 'core Europe' exerting a centrifugal force on Europe's Scandinavian borders?

As Norwegians prepared to vote on their country's entrance into the EU, twenty-eight prominent authors compiled a Eurosceptical anthology; ten thousand volunteers distributed 1.8 million copies of the volume to every household. The book was a call for a left-patriotism, for in areas of democracy and civil rights the EU continues to fall markedly short of Nordic standards. Norway compensated for its EU abstinence through activist foreign and development aid policies. Now, all signs and polls indicate that Norway will enter the Union within the foreseeable future.

Europe – a Necessary Evil

For Scandinavians, Europe is no magic formula but simply a necessary evil, to which there is no alternative. Several days ago the author Carl Henning Wijmark remarked in the pages of the newspaper *Dagens Nyheter* that Sweden's debate over the EU has amounted to a set of 'pecuniary odd jobs,' instead of a debate on belonging to the continent 'to which we owe everything.' Sweden voted for EU entry on September 14,

2002. Finland, a country that experienced a renaissance in the 1990s, is the only Nordic country whose inhabitants have refused the common currency. This should not come as a surprise. A Grand Duchy of Russia from 1809 until 1917, the country was bound to the Soviet Union by a 'treaty of friendship and mutual aid' from the end of the Second World War until the fall of the Iron Curtain.

As debates over the EU constitution have raged over these past weeks and months, the Scandinavian countries, as smaller EU member-states, have been intent on preserving as much of their influence as possible. It is this debate, and not the debate on 'core Europe,' that has been the major topic in the Danish press. 'Core Europe' and a common European foreign policy direct one's attention upwards, toward the perspective of the great powers; in the North, by contrast, a downward-looking perspective predominates: the desire to democratize the EU. Alongside national perspectives, there is also a European perspective, the advent of a European 'we-consciousness.' There is worry that the EU could damage this consciousness if Silvio Berlusconi assumes the office of President of the European Council. An editorial in the Danish newspaper *Politics* accuses Berlusconi of 'disregard for the institutions of the rule of law and democratic decency,' and challenges the EU to name 'a less embarrassing candidate' for the high office.

Closer to America

America lies closer to the heart for many Scandinavians than Europe. Minister-President Anders Fogh Rasmussen, who supported the United States in the Iraq war, has stated in a newspaper article that Denmark's security was guaranteed by the American superpower, rather than 'the fragile balance of power amongst Germany, France, and England.' Denmark, which now counts as a hesitant EU country, was formerly a multicultural state, which once included not just Norway but Iceland, the Faroes, and the duchies of Schleswig and Holstein. Around the year 1700, some 20 per cent of Copenhagen's population was German-speaking, and Herder still regarded Copenhagen as 'the Danish end of Germany.' Up until the end of the eighteenth century, German was the native tongue of the Danish royal family. It was only in 1773 that Danish became the official language of the army.

Young intellectuals took up common cause against German dominance. The hostile image of parasitic Germans, disdaining anything Danish, was embodied in Count Struensee, the court physician of the King (and the Queen's lover), a character recognizable from Per Olov Enquist's novel *The Royal Physician's Visit*.[1] The country was reconfigured as a nation-state over the course of the nineteenth century. Defeated militarily by Prussia and Austria in 1864, Denmark lost a third of its remaining territory. 'What has been lost to the outside must be re-won on the inside' became the motto. The construction of the welfare state in the 1930s demanded domestic cohesion, and immunized the country against anti-democratic threats from the South and the East.

Referring to the Second World War, Jürgen Habermas and Jacques Derrida speak of a 'bellicose past' that 'entangled all European nations in bloody conflicts,' from which Europe has learned its lesson and founded supranational organizations. One may well ask what is meant by Denmark's 'bellicose past.' Hardly the rescue of seven thousand Jews, who in a few October nights in 1943 were able to cross the Øresund and escape deportation thanks to the help of countless Danish citizens.[2]

Neue Zürcher Zeitung, June 14, 2003
Translated by Max Pensky

---

[1] Per Olov Enquist, *The Royal Physician's Visit: A Novel* (Washington Square Press, 2002).

[2] While the Danish government offered no resistance to German occupation in 1940, in 1943 a large number of Danish citizens, alerted to

the impending deportation of Denmark's small Jewish population, saved nearly all Danish Jews by boat, over the narrow Øresund Sound separating Denmark from neutral Sweden.

THE ORGANIZING POWER

Karl Otto Hondrich

The signs in the heavens are unmistakable. The horsemen of the apocalypse are on their way. Under the banner of the Stars and Stripes, on a wild hunt around the globe. They plough through the clouds wherever they wish. Today Iraq is theirs, and tomorrow the entire world. Madness! Those who think like this, however, are not Americans but masters from Germany. The megalomania of power originates in the eye of the beholder. Hitler still haunts our minds. These are his dreams of world domination, which we transfer onto the United States. If one were to believe the augurs of old Europe, then the world knows no greater danger than the predominance of the United States.

Who could resist their arguments? It is true that conflicts should be settled nonviolently, within the scope of the law. The role of bringing the world to order is supposed to fall to the United Nations, not the United States. Yes, up to this point, the power of the world should be distributed in a 'multipolar' manner. As plausible as these requirements seem, they are based on an illusion. Force, not law, is the order that forms the basis of society. In global society, it is the United States and not the UN that builds on this foundation. The distribution of power to multiple poles, even if it were possible, would produce less peace, not more. The tremendous power of the United States is not the problem. It is the solution. But what, then, is the problem?

The problem is the diversity and the global dispersion of violent force. And it's a problem getting worse: increasing numbers of states, gangs, terrorists, and fanatics can get hold of devastating weapons and can spread terror throughout the world. We cannot cope with these threats with rights and contracts. And yet history has provided a solution, although in smaller scope. Here in Europe, a multipolar arrangement, a kind of equal distribution of power among many rulers, led to continual trials of strength. The modern state as a monopolist of power emerged from just these trials. Its hegemony secures peace – a peace, though, only internally.

Competition arises in the external relationships between states once they have become national hegemonies, and with this competition comes an elevated risk of violence. The 'balance of power,' of which modern Europe from Metternich to Bismarck has been so proud, has merely banished violence temporarily, only to collapse in even greater violence. It can only be ascribed to a lucky roll of the dice that the 'balance of terror' between NATO and the Warsaw Pact did not lead to a nuclear inferno. It transformed itself into the dominance of the United States.

None of this goes according to plan, or justice, or law. A legal order that constrains violence according to rules presumes a hegemonic order of violence. Old Europe seems to have forgotten the basic role of violence. It does not feel itself under attack, either by Bin Laden or by Saddam, not by the Hamas commandos nor from the Congo. It would appear that it believes violence is to be conquered not by violence but instead by nonviolence. Is it a coincidence that only the British and the Spanish, who have known terror in their own country, back a violent solution in Iraq?

The less we experience remote violence, understand it and adopt it as a problem, the quicker we have the patent remedy at hand: The UN has to fix it. Yet, it cannot do this. It has no power. Wherever law cannot be imposed, there is no law. What the UN lacks most of all, however, is the force of shared interests and feelings that make collective action in the outside world possible. The UN has no outside and so remains divided on the inside. It sees itself as a whole; tragically, therefore, it is unable to act on behalf of the whole.

The United States has what the United Nations lacks: not a monopoly of world power, but leadership in a cartel of armed powers. What enables it to act – the distinction between good and evil, national and foreign, friend and foe – seems to make it simultaneously incapable of acting for the whole. Even if the UN calls upon it to act, it always remains a nation that is only part of the whole and bound to its own interests. However, as interests of a great power, these can extend much farther than those of other states. They come close to the interests of the whole, at least in matters of protection against violence. Even without a desire for establishing order for the whole (which could well become dangerous) it fulfills a central task, even unintentionally, of all statehood: to keep violence out of the free play of forces and to calm the situation. In the quasi-world-state, this task is immense. Because nobody else undertakes it, the order of world violence is, therefore, perforce, US-hegemonic. Does the task not ask too much from the strength of one nation? The US assumes too much, according to some critics; economically it lives at the expense of others, as it chronically imports more than it exports. One can, however, interpret this quite differently: the world returns to the United States in goods what it obtains in military services.

For a long time, there has been a global division of labor, functioning without contracts or laws, even without justice, and yet somehow it works: people work for the world in Asia, pray for the world in Arabia, suffer for the world in Africa, arm themselves for the world in the United States, and carry on discussions for the world in Europe. All these tasks serve the community in their way. But no amount of discussion and reflection on the legacy of Europe is going to talk a community into existence. In the context of struggle (including the struggle against hunger) community emerges on its own.

As with all power, there are limits on the power of the hegemonic state as well – from outside, through the great powers
of Russia, China, and India. They no longer compete with the
US for control over the whole world (as was the case up to
1989), but compete for their respective spheres of influence.
Yet those powers, particularly Russia, have dramatically
decreased in size; Eastern Europe as a whole has deserted to
the protection of NATO, and even Russia, threatened by
Islamic terrorism and the unleashed industrial dynamic of
China, leans *de facto* towards NATO.

And what if this should one day absorb all powers into a
worldwide security system? It would then also make its external
boundaries into internal ones. Even now, these boundaries
become visible in the resistance of the NATO partners to the
Iraq war. The more encompassing the cartel of violence
becomes, the more fragile is its inner unity, and all the greater
are the concessions that the leading power has to make in order
to achieve the unity and allocation of power.

The greatest limitation of hegemonic power stems from the
innermost core of the hegemon itself. The United States represents the oldest and most popular of modern democracies – a
nation that embraces the notion of popular sovereignty more
than any European people would have ever thought possible.
They do not want to see their soldiers shed their blood on
foreign battlefields. In the long run, they don't want to share
the attentions of their government with Burundi, Berlin or
Baghdad. When it has to handle affairs abroad – 'some business to do,' as going to war is called in American English –
then the United States wants to do so in its own interests, and
not to spread global happiness, as has been pilloried in Europe
since day one. If other peoples get something out of its wars
– freedom and democracy, for example – they are welcome to
them. Americans are proud of it. But the idea that the United
States forces the American Way of Life upon others is ridiculous: what people want to have of their own free will does not
have to be imposed on them through violence.

Nor through money. The American people would much rather invest at home in education, health, and security. If the president fails to provide for these interests, then he'll have to go, as did his father before him. The bigger the projects a hegemonic power undertakes, the sooner it runs up against its financial limits. For this reason alone, it needs both internal and external consent; this is legitimacy. Any opposition increases the risk, the duration, and the costs of a war.

Moreover, this apparently global hegemon does not run the world. In foreign lands, it pulls up short before the spheres of influence of other great powers. Closer to home, the crude club of its weapons of mass destruction is helpless against the violent needling and terror on its own body, in Belfast, San Sebastián, or New York. Its zone of hegemonic control in the world is little more than a medium-range firebreak.

This, however, is too little for those master thinkers of an imaginary global interest, on their cruise on the European ship of dreams. They want order for everyone. They want the United States small and large at the same time. As an aircraft carrier, the United States can't be small enough for them, but as the carrier of an idea of general global welfare, it cannot be far-reaching enough.

But the fact that that the hegemon is a nation, and only a nation – not a global council of wise men, not a non-governmental organization, not the world state – is anything but lamentable. It offers the chance that the hegemon will operate within its own limited interest and not from an unbridled and universal idealism, however many fundamentalist will-o-the-wisps may be flickering away inside it. It can be wrong, as was the case with Vietnam. But there is nothing to indicate that it has thrown overboard the self-limiting reason of national interests. It rests in the experience of an old, mature, unbroken, fundamentally democratic, and multicultural nation. The German experiences of a belated, imperial, perverted, and broken nationalism could not be more contrary. The discrepancy between these experiences cannot be filled, save by mistrust.

Is this not rational? Anchoring hegemony in American democracy surely does not offer a guarantee of everlasting reason. The way US democracy functions in its core, through checks and balances, will need counterweights from the outside as well. The enigmatic concept of 'multipolarity' stands precisely for that. It can mean a lot of things: a reality, a nice pretense, or simply stupidity.

The large and small poles that crystallize from power relations are real. In relation to their former colonies, France and Belgium form a pole of power; thus, it is only a logical conclusion that an EU-garrison goes into the Congo under their leadership. The Balkan states depend on Germany and make it unwillingly into a power pole of its own. Seen in this way, multipolarity is in fact already at hand.

But multipolarity turns into a lovely mirage if it causes us to forget that as an internal allocation of power, it is a component of a larger hegemonic system. The hegemon relies on it, and vice versa. France, Great Britain, and Germany subjugate and are subjugated at the same time. They are part of a collective hegemony. They explain to those out there in the South and the East the sorts of ugly things that threaten if they resist the hegemon. Conversely, they explain to the hegemon the fears and resistances of the rest of the world. From its point of view, the Europeans remain, at the same time, minor devils, as long as they participate in the punishment, and demi-gods in white, because they do so with understanding, and send along hospital ships. Thus, they find their function: as facilitators between supremacy and impotence.

The hegemonic system is already so powerful that it grants great freedoms both externally and internally. One can either go along with a campaign of the hegemon or not. Even without a parliament, the system creates a kind of extra-parliamentary opposition for itself: Gerhard Schröder's Germany and the France of Jacques Chirac – with Habermas, Derrida, and Rorty up their sleeves – are the extra-parliamentary opposition to George W. Bush's America. The '68ers can use the arsenal of old arguments: the danger and villainy of America, the dangers to democracy and the constitutional state. Is all this just the same old anti-Americanism? It is far more opposition within our very own Atlantic house. The Germans have finally arrived in the West. Too bad that the West has turned out to be not just an open society, but a shell casing for hegemony as well.

The Germans can no longer get out of this. Should they nevertheless dream of a European home of their own, ignoring the reality that such a home, in isolation, would be poised on the edge of an abyss? I am afraid that this is exactly what they have in mind: Europe as a power pole beyond US hegemony that would, in concert with others, i.e., with Poland, Russia, China, India, and Africa, abolish hegemony? 'Multipolarity' would be the first step in the project to achieve progress that would prove to be a step backward (see socialism). It would, however, be by far the most foolish and dangerous one. It would lead us back into new dimensions of old, violent competitive battles that we have put behind us. Thanks to US hegemony. May that frog stay stuck in our throat.

Der Spiegel, June 16, 2003

BETWEEN SOVEREIGNTY AND HUMAN RIGHTS:
Juxtaposing American and European Tradition

Dan Diner

In the year 1853, German democrats in exile in the United States published a manifesto that created a sensation. Their call to action carried the title 'The New Rome, or the United States of the World,' and it asked the United States to intervene in Europe. The objective was the establishment of a World Republic. The manifesto culminated in a call to combat tyranny everywhere.

From its very inception, the American Project was committed to a revolutionary predilection. Prince Metternich knew what he was talking about when he declared a battle of 'altar against altar,' in the name of the European restoration on the model of the doctrine named after the American President Monroe. Actually, this explanation did not conceal its extreme anti-monarchical, anti-despotic, democratic and free-trade character. In 1848, when the United States of America honored the Saint Paul's Church Assembly in Frankfurt with an ambassador appointed solely for this event, the signs had been posted: The New World represented a new time.

The United States was deeply sceptical of the European order of powers and the law of nations emanating from Europe. Not until the end of the nineteenth century did America elevate its *chargés d'affaires,* who were stationed in the capital cities of Europe, to the rank of ambassador. According to the American interpretation of the law, the modern European law of nations basically served the *status quo* of the old order – a modern *Cuius regio eius religio*. Its most noble objective was the security of peace, independent from this or that conception of justice. This status was supported by a system of balance among the powers themselves that increasingly came to be formalized in the principle of the balance of power between them. The United States had no part in this European principle of a 'multi-laterally' structured balance of power.

Crusade for Freedom

The Prussian reformist Lorenz von Stein had called attention to a significant difference between the legal tradition of the law of nations arising from the continent and the Anglo-Saxon tradition of 'International Law.' The former he found to be based on a territorial juxtaposition of subjects of the state with equal rights under international law, the latter on legal maxims justified by a sense of humanity. International laws have a 'vertical' effect because they universally seek to infiltrate the territoriality and sovereignty imposed by the state. In this respect, they are interventionist by their very nature. In legal practice, horizontally and vertically structured constructions intermingle – whereby the United States, as a 'bourgeois society without state' (Hegel), grants priority to universal legal principles. Following tradition and inclination, there are thus two kinds of legal construction, working in opposite directions: in Europe the priority of the territorially limiting state; in the United States the priority of an unbounded society.

The American understanding of war is analogous to this distinction – in essence, a war of values that is inherently different from the old-European tradition of war between states. There are historical sources for this. America had sprung from a civil war: the rebellion of North American colonists against the English King over the principle of representation. This was followed by the internal American Civil War, a war overtly about values. The United States entered the First World War, in Wilson's own words, 'in order to make the world safe for democracy.' Then came the Second World War as a 'crusade

for freedom,' followed by the Cold War, which was a cosmopolitan war of values contrasting freedom and Communism.

The globally provoked entrance of the United States into
two world wars that were caused by Europe had struck the
continental tradition of the law of nations in its heart. For
decades, the opposition of superpowers had regulated all
conflicts; through a balance of terror, it had guaranteed something like equality of security. With the fall of the Soviet Union
and the worldwide achievement of a world market, characterized as globalization, there was 'an extension of bourgeois
society beyond the state' (Marx), something like a formal affinity
between transnational socialization and the hegemonic imposition of the principle of 'America' as just this bourgeois society
without a state – an 'imperial republic' (Raymond Aron).

The global reactions of the United States in response to the
events of September 11 revealed the anachronistic features of
a law of nations that remains shaped by old-European ideas of
territoriality. In order to put an end to the violence of trans-
territorial terrorism; in order to make the United States safe
in particular, the ambiguities of isolationism and interven-
tionism were abolished in American foreign policy. The United
States acts like what it has always been: a hegemon of world
society without a home.

America's unilateral military action has been charged with
illegality and illegitimacy in the framework of international
law; according to an oft-proclaimed, hackneyed view, it shattered the framework of international law itself. But what was
shattered was a hollow shell of institutions of international law,
dedicated to legitimizing the actions of member nations, such
as the UN Security Council, that arose in the aftermath of the
Second World War. These institutions thus symbolically
prolonged an old order of states that had already been proven
wrong militarily some sixty years ago. Thus France was
rewarded with a seat in the Security Council as a symbolic
gesture, just as it had received its occupation zone in Germany:
borrowed power, an act of the United States' largesse, driven

by thoughts of prestige without any real cover. In the Iraq crisis, it was precisely this historical privilege which France exercised through its veto right in the procedural prerogative to decide, finally, whether military action against the regime of Saddam Hussein would be legal under international law, regardless of whatever the political intentions of the United States might be. It was an open secret that one goal behind the veil of a debate on quasi-international law ultimately was the promotion of a multilateral world against America.

Cries about America's breach of international law are reminiscent of the complaints of jurists and public opinion in reaction to the Nuremberg Trials in Germany in 1946. The legal protection of *nulla poena sine lege* (no punishment without a corresponding law) was held up like a trophy of legal certainty that covers over all the horrors, in contrast to the Anglo-Saxon concept of law, which regarded criminal behavior as punishable even in cases where commissions of such acts had not been codified according to positive law.

International law needs to be developed further. And this is a good thing. In this respect, it will not be possible to avoid recognizing something like a substantial prerogative for the 'American' variant of human rights that vertically penetrates the sovereignty of individual states. After all, in his essay on 'Perpetual Peace,' Kant had already presupposed a beneficent international order, not merely an arbitrary plethora of states constituted no matter how, but in terms of 'republics' – that is, of democracies.

Süddeutsche Zeitung, June 16, 2003

A GREAT INNOVATION
OF OUR TIMES:
As a Worldwide Recognized Role Model, Europe Does Not Need a Constitution

Dieter Grimm

Shortly after the eleventh hour, the European Convention submitted the draft of a European Constitution. It is not yet fully completed. Doubtless, however, the final gaps will be filled shortly; doubtless the draft will soon be completed; and doubtless it will then lead the European Union a good deal further on its way from a common market to a political union. There is little doubt that the conference of heads of states and the governments of the member nations will accept the draft, even though probably not without amendments. The text unanimously decided by the intergovernmental conference then has to be ratified by the member states according to the rules of their national constitutions, and goes into force as soon as all ratification documents have been submitted.

Many things, however, speak for the fact that this draft – despite its identification as 'constitution,' that has by now asserted itself against the initially chosen concept 'constitutional treaty' – is not about a constitution but would, after all, be a constitutional treaty. This is a substantive, not just a formal distinction. Fundamentally, it is about who is allowed to determine the basic legal order of the Union: the member-states, by negotiating its content, or the European Union, by granting itself by means of a decision of the responsible organ a basic order with or without referendum.

Of course, the member states are not prevented from giving away the final responsibility for the Union at the intergovernmental conference and handing it over to the Union itself. An international treaty with this effect would then be the last one concerning the basic order of the Union. After this contract the Union would be free to amend or to reform its basic order at its own discretion. The member-states could still be involved in decisions of this sort, although no longer as the bearers of the European Union, but as members of one of its organs. In fact, this does not seem to be what is meant to happen, for, according to the draft of the constitution, the governmental conference (which is not an organ of the Union) and the peoples or the representative bodies of the member-states will have the final word in matters concerning the basic legal order.

The document that is called the 'constitution' therefore lacks one essential element of a true constitution in the full sense of the concept. It is not the expression of self-determination of a sovereign European people, but refers back to an act of heteronomy on the part of the member-states. This is anything but a matter of formality. Significant consequences arise out of this discrepancy. If, regardless of the designation 'constitution,' the text remains a treaty, this means that the Union will continue not to be a self-supporting organization, but will remain a construct borne by the member-states. As a result, it does not have the right to take responsibilities away from its member-states. They must instead be granted to it.

There is, however, no reason to regret this, because the expectations that are linked to a real constitution would scarcely be fulfilled. The fact that many people wish for a constitution along the lines of a model for a national state cannot be explained by the indisputable need for reform of the European Union. All reforms that are held to be necessary – the adaptation of organs and procedures appropriate to the deepened integration and the expanded number of members, the facilitation of a common foreign and security policy, the establishment of a presidential office, the transfer of the Charter of basic rights into binding law – can be achieved within the scope of the treaties. One does not need a constitution to do these things.

With the constitution certain goals are pursued that go beyond institutional reform. On the one hand, it is hoped that a constitution will cover the European democratic deficit that has long been a source of complaint. On the other hand one hopes that it will bridge the gap between citizens of the Union and the European institutions as well as overcome the indifference felt by most Europeans towards the Union, which is rapidly proving to be an obstacle to the integration in progress. Unlike a treaty, the constitution is not only supposed to spread its effects on a judicial but also on a symbolic level; furthermore, it is supposed to anchor the European Union in the hearts of the citizens, forming as well the crystallization point for a European identity.

The surrender of the final responsibility of the member-states and the transition to a self-supporting Union would, of course, only be defensible if the expected reward were in fact to take place with a certain degree of probability and if the Union, after being constitutionalized, were to be more democratic and closer to the people than before. Yet this seems quite doubtful. The deficit in democracy has its actual basis not in the fact that its organs lack the same democratic legitimation and full competencies that the national state constitutions provide. The fundamental cause lies rather in the fact that up to this point the European Union has not rested on a basis that is sufficiently solid for a self-supporting organization in democratic terms.

Democracy is not exhausted by the periodic election of a parliament or a president, as long as one understands it not just formally but rather substantially. What is decisive is the social context in which the basic democratic act is embedded. If democracy is understood as the relationship of mandate and responsibility between the people and the organs that act in its name, then everything depends on whether or not society is in a position to communicate discursively about its own affairs, to integrate its interests and convictions into the political process between elections, and to make the responsibility of the governing bodies real.

These social preconditions of democracy are more or less well developed in the nation-states. In Europe they are still absent to a great extent. A European public sphere and a Europe-wide discourse – which is not merely the sum of fifteen, soon to be twenty-five, national discourses – exist only at the level of elites. But democracy is not an event for the elite but an event for all. Those communications media that would be in a position to provide a context for the European discussion are only to be found in specialist publications and not in the general mass communication field that is accessible to everyone. And, in the face of growing language barriers, one cannot count on any rapid change in this condition.

This does not mean that democracy is not worth any further effort at a European level. In fact, quite the opposite holds true. In this respect, the European Parliament plays a leading role because it can bring together national discourses, foster the formation of a European party system, make today's predominantly gubernatorial-bureaucratic decision-making practices more transparent, and form a counterbalance to the influence of interested parties and experts. With good reason it has therefore been strengthened in the constitution drafted by the Convention. However, as part of the European structure of governing, it is not in a position to replace the missing societal preconditions of a vigorous democratic exchange process.

It is just as unlikely that a European Constitution would develop the identity-founding momentum that successful national-state constitutions such as the German Basic Law possess. After all that one knows about constitutions which have acquired a symbolic effect surmounting the content of their judicial regulation, it is clear that they arise out of an exceptional situation: a triumphant revolution or a nation's rise after a catastrophic defeat has been carved into the collective memory, something that is recalled in the constitution and is, thus, in a position to keep alive that kind of solidarity and the willingness to make sacrifices that differentiates a political unity from a mere partnership of convenience.

In Europe there is, at present, no such 'constitutional moment,' as Bruce Ackermann has called it. Under these circumstances, even a real constitution that is ascribed to the European people instead of one decided by the member-states is only another step on the path to an integration, driven forward by gubernatorial, administrative, and judicial forces. Even the circumstances cannot alter the fact that the text has been designed this time by an advisory panel that is only partly identical with the participants of the political agenda in Brussels and the national capital cities, and which enjoys greater sympathy than the usual summit conferences which in the past have added new layers to the treaties with constantly growing difficulty.

Admittedly, it is all the more important to give an account of what the sense and particular nature of the European Union consists in. Only on the basis of such assurances can Europe develop further in a more single-minded way and position itself with respect to its environment. The settlement of hostile conflicts that have devastated Europe for centuries was present at its very beginning, and the space of peace that has developed in this way belongs, to this day, among the greatest achievements of European unification. Meanwhile, however, the European Union no longer assuages yearnings, but is rather taken for granted in Europe. On this basis the need for additional justifications for the European project can also be explained.

If the EU is supposed to grow further beyond an economic community and strive forward into a political community, it must do so on the basis of common values that are not exhausted in material prosperity. In this respect, especially worth considering are human rights, democracy, the rule of law, welfare provision or solidarity, pluralism, and the enhancement of culture. The draft of the Convention names them all in Article I-2 in reference to the 'values of the Union,' with the exception of culture, which was only mentioned later. They are of European origin, yet they are not restricted to Europe any

100 OLD EUROPE, NEW EUROPE, CORE EUROPE

longer; instead they are today considered values of the 'West' and even claim, to a growing degree, a universal prestige.

Europe shares them particularly with America, where these values were first and permanently secured in a constitution. Both stand equally in the 'Western' tradition. For this reason, it is not to be recommended that we understand European identity as an alternative to the Atlantic attachment, as Jürgen Habermas has suggested (*Frankfurter Allgemeine Zeitung* of May 31). There are, of course, different understandings and accentuations of these values on both sides of the Atlantic, differences that had faded into the background during the time of the East–West opposition and the Communist threat, but which have become once again more noticeable. Such differences on a concrete level exist, of course, within Europe as well. Some of these differences form barriers to further unification, but they do not endanger the project of the European Union.

Just as these differences do not frustrate understanding between European states, they can also be turned into a fruitful dialogue with the United States. The differences of power, though, should not be masked. Whereas there are greater and smaller states in Europe, but no dominating power, the United States has been, since the collapse of the Soviet Union, in a hegemonic position. Admittedly, the transatlantic dialogue does not have to fail because of this. On the contrary, it appears particularly urgent when America, because of its hegemony, is tempted to divest itself of those values in pursuit of its foreign and security policies. The preconditions for equal dialogue, however, will not be created until Europe decides to build up a military power on its side that would come close to that of the United States. Yet, a willingness to spend this much for military power is nowhere to be found. The field is conceded to America. This cannot be without consequences for the transatlantic relationship.

On the other hand, it would be a false goal to seek the European future in creating a United States of Europe in analogous to the United States of America. Many cannot

imagine any other result of European unification. They view
the current confederation, therefore, only as a transitional stage
to a federal state. Yet, it becomes visible everywhere that the
states yield or lose their attribute (namely sovereignty) with
growing globalization and that they open up to binding political decisions that originate from sources of law other than their
own national sources. Although the states will not be absorbed
into a new political order for the time being, they may yet lose
in terms of exclusiveness and significance.

Even a European federal state would not be immune to this
kind of development. Therefore, the hope is unrealistic that
shrinking statehood on the national level could be re-estab-
lished on a higher European level. With a European state, one
is therefore betting on a model from the past. On the other
hand, one can, with good reason, claim that the European
Union presents the most significant political innovation of the
twentieth century. It does not dissolve the national states with
their otherwise irreplaceable resources of legitimacy and solidarity but rather uses them in order to provide solutions for
those kinds of problems that can overtax national powers.

It is precisely this unprecedented formation that can serve
as a model for other parts of the world, as indeed it has already
begun to. This holds especially true for regions that likewise
have rid themselves of deeply rooted often hostile conflicts,
and now wish to increase their productive capacity through
cooperation without sacrificing to this goal their traditions,
characteristics, and predilections. The European Union is
ingeniously devised for this purpose. Although its basic structure needs various adjustments and improvements because of
the sheer number of members it attracts, a convergence to the
nation-state model is not necessary.

This realization also speaks against a European Constitution
in the full meaning of the concept. A Constitution would
detach the basic legal order of the Union from its provision
via the member-states and would transfer it to the self-determination of the Union. In so doing, whether intentionally or

not, the Union would be stripped of its innovative character and turned into a traditional federal state. For, in regards to the basic legal order, it is between heteronomy and self-determination that the fine border of the state and a supranational organization runs. Here and there one might perhaps have expected a bit more from the European Convention. But in this respect it did not allow itself to be seduced, and rightly so.

Frankfurter Allgemeine Zeitung, June 16, 2003

WILD, CUNNING, EXOTIC:

The East Will Completely Shake Up Europe

Andrzej Stasiuk

Albanians, Bosnians, Bulgarians, Estonians, Croatians, Lithuanians, Macedonians, Moldavians, Montenegrins, Poles, Romanians, Serbs, Slovaks, Slovenians, Czechs, Ukrainians, White Russians – this is, more or less, how one might describe the map of the territory of two hundred million future Europeans. And just so it doesn't appear too simple, let's add the 'belt of mixed population' – as Hannah Arendt called the diverse, amorphous areas somewhere between Germany and Russia – that is, small heaps of Germans and Russians scattered here and there. To this, we can add, for example, the Gagausians and Aromunians, the restless international Sinti, the Crimeans and the Turks who didn't get back to their native lands on the Bosporus before it unexpectedly shrank.

Two hundred million new Europeans: that is indeed a real challenge, likely to rob one of a good night's sleep, to provoke anxiety. But joy too, because the events that are about to take place are reminiscent of the discovery of a new continent.

The plan for the coming decades looks more or less like this: the Sinti will arrive with their wagons and will set up camp in the middle of the Champs-Elysées; Bulgarian bears will perform their tricks on Berlin's Kudamm; half-wild Ukrainians will encamp their misogynistic Cossack troops on the plain of the Po before the gates of Milan; drunken Poles rapt in prayer will ravage the vineyards of the Rhine and Mosel and will plant bushes that bear fruit full of pure denatured alcohol and then move on; they will sing their litanies and will not stop until they reach the edge of the continent in the arch-Catholic Santiago de Compostela, famous for its miracles. It is difficult to say what the Romanians will do with their millions of sheep. They are a people known especially for their sheep breeding, but also for their unpredictability. Serbs, Croatians, and Bosnians will cross the English Channel in Dalmatian dugout canoes and Balkanize Britain, which will finally be divided, as God commanded it, into Scotland, England and Wales.

Waiting for the Barbarians

The inhabitants of Latvia and Lithuania will craftily change their identity over and over again and will fool a public accustomed to transparent relations. Slovenians and Slovaks will pass themselves off as inhabitants of Slavonia and will proceed to drive computer systems in the entire EU into despair. Moldavians whose main source of income comes from selling their own organs (as a certain newspaper in Germany has reported) will metamorphose as an entire people into clinking coins and ruin the world market of transplants. And what the Albanians will do exceeds any human powers of imagination …

A friend of mine, the outstanding Ukrainian prose writer and lyricist Jurij Andruchowycz, once said that an author coming from Central or Eastern Europe to the West will find an ideal literary situation there. He can narrate fantastic stories about his country, about his part of the continent, can sell them as nothing but the truth and can then retire comfortably because his stories will never be verified. This is possible, on the one hand, because the public thinks that just about anything could indeed happen here; on the other hand, because these countries remind the West more of literary fiction than of actually existing states.

The immediate future of Europe will be the encounter with fiction, a fiction populated by two hundred million extremely real creatures. In this situation, disagreements carried out in Paris, Berlin or London appear somehow anachronistic. The continent will soon change until it is totally unrecognizable, and nothing will be as it once was. I have no intention of ascribing a certain potential to the Moldavians, Poles or Central European Gypsies. I simply try to see this part of the world as a whole that will change the face of the continent, even if only by virtue of its idleness. These peculiar, uncanny, exotic tribes will find themselves in Europe once more. However, it would be naive to believe that they will give up their customs and bad habits, their boisterous needs, their phantasms and traumata, their specific temperament – in short, that they will forgo their individual characteristics for the benefit of some liberal, democratic European universalities. Their situation resembles that of barbaric conquerors to whom the gates were opened, as this was the only solution. Do you remember the poem by Konstantinos Kavafi entitled 'Waiting for the Barbarians'?

Thus, a long, nice ending heralds their coming. It will take some time before the new tribes, which emerge out of nothing, will have eaten their fill of prey, until they have digested it and adapted it to their own situation, perfected and, finally, converted it into a parody of themselves. Yet, before that happens, old Europe will go through its second adolescence. While forfeiting its success in the world, it will regain it in its own eyes after a time. It will be able to export prosperity, security, order, contentment, and exclusivity, as it has exported cars, clothes, and food up to now. Certainly, this multi-layered, sensitive non-materialistic commodity will need modification to satisfy the unpredictable tastes of this unknown people; its attractiveness will need constant enhancement. At least as long as the most remote edges of the continent do not master the secrets of independent production.

It is not out of the question that old Europe might no longer be needed by then. In the absence of any more meaningful activity, it will occupy itself with its own history and will reminisce over its former importance. In a paradoxical way, it will repeat the destiny of its younger sister ('new' Europe), which only recently had been thoroughly preoccupied with its very own history, which, alas, consisted of a chain of defeats, disappointments, and injustices of fate. Old Europe will also share the lot of its younger sister in the experience of the feeling of redundancy. Debtors very rarely show gratitude. As soon as they get back on their feet, they will ascribe all the achievements to themselves and their memory will miraculously erase that time of humiliation.

Can one unite two currents of history that have flowed in separate, parallel courses for so long, especially when one current seemed to vanish underground whenever the other accelerated? Peoples never remember a common history, but approach each other from their own unique history. It is like that with the future too. We can plan it as our common future, but as soon as it arrives, it will metamorphose on the spot into the past, and then it is only our personal property, because it is the only thing we have.

Süddeutsche Zeitung, June 20, 2003

THE DAY OF THE KNOW-IT-ALLS

Peter Schneider

The war in Iraq has been won; the peace has not yet begun.
In the chaotic transitional period, supporters as well as opponents of the invasion seek to justify their arguments. The fact
that the protagonists on both sides feel themselves fully
confirmed by the course of the war is a part of the war's many
surprises. 'We were right,' the call echoes from the White House
across to Europe; 'We were the far-sighted ones,' Klaus Staeck[1]
calls back in the name of millions of German opponents of
the war. The paradoxical spectacle can only be explained by
the fact that the spokespersons remind us only of the predictions that seem to have been confirmed by events, and are
determined to forget all the ones that have been refuted.

What concerns the strategists of the coalition partners
America and Great Britain is that one of their most vehemently
disputed assumptions has been proven right. The war against
the Iraqi dictator was not only swift, but was also a surpris-
ingly bloodless victory. The rapid victory has further revealed
overwhelming evidence in support of an accusation presented
by Tony Blair that had been dismissed by many opponents of
the war as horror propaganda: namely, we have dealt with
Saddam Hussein's regime not as a kind of dictatorship but as
one of the most horrible tyrannies in more recent history.

Anyone who has read the corresponding reports and still has
the heart to shrug his shoulders, pointing to the many other
dictatorships in the world, is a scoundrel, and by her behavior

shows that condemning the United States is more important than the destiny of those deprived of their rights, in whose name she believes she speaks. Whatever may come after the victory of the coalition will definitely be more endurable than Saddam's reign of terror.

But what about the other announcements and promises made by those proud victors from the White House and Downing Street? No evidence has been found for the official reason of war: namely the existence and production of weapons of mass destruction in Iraq. It is becoming increasingly obvious that the global public of the warlords, who obviously rely on the reports of agitators in their secret services – or even on willing helpers? – has been deceived. Such an accusation made toward two leaders of the West, who appeal to morality in every other sentence, is no trivial thing and must have repercussions in a democracy. The worst of all, however, is that the liberators had taken great care in preparation for the war, but have prepared for the postwar period like amateurs, and even now are in danger of losing the peace.

In one respect, all opponents of the war in this world are correct: the war against Iraq was a decision made long before the actual war; it had little or nothing to do with a current threat to the United States by Iraqi weapons of mass destruction, and probably not all that much to do with 'humanitarian intervention.' It was, according to the yardstick of the law of nations at that time, a war in defiance of international law, and the global community never had a serious chance to avert it.

But what about the remaining arguments and predictions of the opponents of the war? The Minister of the Environment, Jürgen Trittin, predicted twenty to forty thousand war victims in an attack on Iraq. Angelika Beer[2] was sure that the entire Near East would explode. Peter Scholl-Latour,[3] the *éminence grise* of the doom-sayers, had gone on record even before the war against Afghanistan, saying that the Americans had not won any war since the Second World War. For the Iraq war he prophesied burning oil fields and house-to-house combat lasting for years. Despite such – how should one put it politely – extremely visionary prognoses, Scholl-Latour has been and remains an eagerly sought-after talk-show guest. In the weeks before the beginning of the Iraq war, he could sometimes be seen on two or three channels at the same time. Obviously, he says what many Germans want to hear, against all evidence and better information. One may rest assured that no one will remind him of this prediction when, once again, it turns out to be false – as I venture to predict it will be.

I lived in Washington, DC in the weeks before and during the war. This coincidence has confirmed my initial opposition against the Bush War rather than soothed it, though I certainly know only bad reasons, not good ones, why cruel tyrants such as Saddam Hussein shouldn't be overthrown, whether through diplomatic or military means.

Nevertheless, I was against this war – for one reason in particular: because the warlord was George W. Bush and because he leads the most radical, anti-liberal government his country has ever seen.

When one lives in the heart of a capital city prosecuting a war, one's senses become sharpened for the domestic political fallout of a 'war of liberation.' What one sees is not an orchestrated but rather a voluntary transformation of news media into instruments of government propaganda; the shameless panic-mongering of the newly created, gigantic bureaucracy of 'homeland security'; the detention of numerous American citizens of Arabic origin and the refusal of their right to see a lawyer; and the primitive anti-European rabble-rousing of the media.

But any opponent of the war, no matter on which side of the Atlantic or for what reasons she raised her voice, suddenly faced a choice when the war started. She had to decide how far she wanted to go in her rejection of an Anglo-American invasion. Was she supposed to rejoice clandestinely or even publicly when the advance of the coalition forces seemed to be halted in the South by Iraqi militia after only a few days?

Should she even cross her fingers for the Iraqi army and the militiamen and congratulate them for each American helicopter shot down? Should she wish that they kill or capture as many of the attackers as possible? Or, after the invasion was no longer avoidable, ought she to wish success to the troops of the coalition and hope that they reach Baghdad and topple the tyrant as quickly and with as little loss of life as possible among the civilian population and within their own ranks?

The decision for the second option was inevitably followed by a further decision: the answer to the question of what óne actually considers worse – Saddam Hussein's regime of terror or George W. Bush's America, which had set out to remove the tyrant from power, for whatever reasons.

My impression is that, in this matter, most of the German opponents of the war either made no decision at all, or decided that the United States was by far the greater evil. Much of what I read in those days about the grotesquely exaggerated or simply falsified Anglo-American intelligence about Saddam Hussein's weapons program irritates me. I share this indignation, but I also hear a false undertone. The impression arises that the greatest crime, the 'actual' crime, in the region was the American invasion and possibly not the regime of the mass murderer Saddam.

Yet, beyond the all the false reasons offered up as evidence, weren't there also a few good reasons for this war? Disregarding the question of legitimacy for a moment, is it a good or a bad thing if democracies liberate a people from a tyrant that they were demonstrably unable to get rid of on their own? And what is the basis for the firm conviction of so many Germans that the ambitious project of an imported democracy that worked so well with themselves could never succeed among Arabs?

One might object that the Crusaders from the Pentagon have interests in mind other than human rights in Iraq. I do not deny this. But from the standpoint of a political prisoner in Iraq, that objection, as Adam Michnik responded,[4] is quite trivial. Whether or not it was a liberal or a neo-conservative American government that liberated him means very little. It does happen in history that the wrong people do the right thing for highly dubious reasons. And then there remains the problem for many peace-lovers who see the war only from the perspective of their rage against the American aggressor and not from the perspective of the victims of Saddam Hussein's dictatorship.

What is really more important: the well-being of the Iraqi citizens or the well-being of one's own preconceived convictions?

The unprecedented unanimity that took shape against the Iraq war, especially in Germany (unlike in the case of the Vietnam War), had something anxiety-provoking about it. Shortly before the beginning of the war, hundreds of authors, artists, and scientists, especially those in Germany, made yet another appeal to the general public against the war. At this point, all surveys revealed that 80 to 90 percent of Germans approved of their position. How much bravery and civil courage did it actually take to let the warning voice of the intellectuals be heard once again in such an environment? Wasn't 90 percent agreement enough? Did the remaining 10 percent of Germans have to be convinced too?

In a speech delivered in Halle, Günter Grass named one of the motives for not leaving well enough alone, one with particular resonance for this majoritarian mood: 'People have often asked us Germans if we are proud of our country. The answer did not come easily. And there were reasons for our hesitation. I can say, however, that the rejection by the majority of the citizens of my country of the preventive war that has just begun made me a little proud of Germany ... For the first time, the government made use of this sovereignty (acquired in 1990), by having the courage to contradict the powerful ally ...'[5]

And not a word about the criminal regime that was the object of this preventive war? Did it require a cry of protest against the United States by 90 percent of the German throats against our former liberator, in order to rediscover that 'pride in being German?' I would have preferred to name other reasons in order to provide examples for my modestly defined pride, such as the decision of the Socialist–Green coalition to participate in the NATO intervention to end ethnic cleansing in Kosovo, for example – this, by the way, was also not legitimized by the UN.

The tasks with which the precarious war in Iraq confronts Western democracies demand a few uncomfortable insights from the self-righteous on both sides. Nothing would be worse than if the Americans, having taken this mission on themselves, were to withdraw as quickly as possible from Iraq after their victory. With the rebuilding of an Iraq ravaged by dictatorship and war, the victors will be in urgent need of these reviled war objectors from Europe. In the Balkans as in Afghanistan, we have seen that the Europeans summon up more patience and sympathy for the rebuilding of civil structures than the allies from overseas; furthermore, the Europeans can fall back on intellectual and cultural resources that others lack.

Jürgen Habermas has elaborated on the cultural and historical differences between Europe and the United States in a manifesto, and has made a remarkable suggestion. Those European pioneer countries, in particular, which provided the initiative for an economic unification some fifty years ago, should now unite into a political union and by doing so create a model for the rest of Europe. Here let me just say that a similar discussion about these differences is taking place in the United States that formulates the question much more brutally. Is there still any common ground at all between Europe and the United States? And even if it still exists, why should anyone be seriously interested in it?

The presumptuous and self-righteous style of the current American administration should be taken by the Europeans as an opportunity for finally giving themselves a political profile. The first condition for this qualitative leap would, of course, be to get rid of a division of labor from which Europe presently draws a lot of false self-confidence: when it really matters, we say, the Americans only understand shooting and bombing; afterward we send in the paramedics and take care of the reconstruction. The conviction that the 'evil' of which the Americans so like to speak may only be an American obsession is, it goes without saying, a European illusion. A new Europe with the old division of labor would only be the old, know-it-all, garrulous and impotent Europe.

Der Spiegel, June 23, 2003

---

[1] Klaus Staeck is a barrister, graphic artist, and political activist; his artistic work includes political posters and placards, as in this reference.

[2] Angelika Beer is a Member of the German Bundestag representing the Green Party and an expert on issues of disarmament.

[3] Peter Scholl-Latour is a prominent German print and television journalist and has published widely on issues of war and peace in the Middle East. His most recent work is *Kampf zum Terror – Kampf zum Islam?* (2002).

[4] Adam Michnik is an influential Polish essayist and journalist, a prominent dissident during the Solidarity Movement in Poland, and the founder and editor of the Polish daily *Gazeta Wyborcza*.

[5] The comments of novelist Günter Grass appeared as 'The U.S. Betrays its Core Values,' *Los Angeles Times*, April 7, 2003.

HABERMAS HAS TOO MUCH CONFIDENCE IN EUROPE

Joachim Starbatty

Jürgen Habermas doesn't just want to interpret the world; he wants to change it. He has launched an initiative, and Europe's leading intellectuals have taken up his concept in the leading newspapers of their respective countries. He has proposed that Europe must become a counterbalance to the United States. He wants to instigate discourse all over Europe that will have an impact on public consciousness and, ultimately, on state policy as well. There is a history leading up to his initiative. On April 17, he worked out analytically the causes and consequences of the Iraq war. About two years ago, he presented in *Die Zeit* the picture of a future Europe.[1] His agenda was, appropriately enough for the subject at hand, a mixture of analytical and normative propositions. His call of May 31 is in principle a synthesis of these two texts; thus, the decisive propositions are again normative: 'Europe must bring its weight to bear on an international level, and within the scope of the UN, in order to balance the hegemonic unilateralism of the United States.' But the demand that Europe has to do something must be preceded by the diagnosis indicating whether or not a containment of hegemony is even necessary, and whether or not Europe can accomplish it.

In the language of the economists, we can see world peace as a collective good, from whose benefits nobody can be excluded. Yet there will always be rulers or regimes seeking national advantage through the violation of peace. In order to prevent such violations, one needs either a hegemon, which by virtue of its economic and political or military power can push for peaceful behavior and punish disruptive behavior, or a proven system of sanctions to which a group of countries agree. Sanctions are then mutually agreed upon; members can be entrusted with punitive actions. This procedure, too, assumes that there are one or more nations to which the character of a hegemon can be awarded. A group of weak countries would not be capable of making credible threats of sanctions. All participants must defer to common dicta.

Because the United States has released itself from this principle, and instituted the Iraq war without the supporting vote of the UN Security Council, Habermas sees the Council's authority in ruins. This view is not shared in the United States; in this newspaper there have been divergent views as well. From an American point of view, it is not the United States that broke international law; it is rather the members of the Security Council, who like to play the role of the anti-hegemon, and would exploit this situation for their own purposes. From this perspective, then, it is the normative authority of the Security Council that lies in ruins. A former American soldier, Ralph Peters, expressed this opinion in this newspaper (*Frankfurter Allgemeine Zeitung* of May 15) in an unvarnished and provocative manner. As a consequence, he did not initiate a discussion but, instead, set loose a flood of emotional letters to the editors; the range of these reaching from 'horrified' and 'disgusted' to 'the truth at last.'

Like Wolves

If one disregards Peters's polemical jabs, then the American position boils down to this: the United States feels abandoned by its allies. Moreover, it has the feeling that these nations are holding the United States back from the pursuit of a just cause; it no longer wants to tolerate this in the future. America does not care whether or not Europeans regard its actions as a breach of international law.

we dont need to care

we are hegemons

From a theoretical point of view, one should now ask the question whether 'world peace,' which is in the collective interest, might not be better assured when it is dependent on the unquestionable authority of a hegemon. This possibility cannot be excluded *a priori*. Therefore, if we see the United States slip into the role of *Paterfamilias* or the benevolent dictator, then we act in the Hobbesian tradition, in which the central power has to secure peace since otherwise men would fall on one another like wolves. Even those who lean toward such a point of view would have to agree, with some hesitation, that the President of the United States appears to think in the Manichean categories of a struggle between good and evil powers. The hegemon might also have a disposition for political adventure whenever its military superiority is too obvious; or it may not accurately assess the consequences of its actions. It is the legacy of the great liberal thinker Friedrich A. von Hayek that we cannot predict with sufficient certainty the consequences of our social actions in a world of uncertainty. Seen from this perspective, we may feel better if either the hegemon submits to some regulation, or if it is counterbalanced by an anti-hegemon.

A potential anti-hegemon must not only muster the will to engage in geopolitics; it must also be prepared to shoulder a significantly higher financial burden for military expenditures and to pay a potentially high toll in blood. A corresponding economic basis is, of course, required in any case. An earlier empirical study of the distribution of power at world economic summits (1978, 1982, and 1987) is informative. It revealed a clear displacement of power away from the United States, and towards Japan and Germany. The increasing economic power of Japan and Germany transferred the power monopoly of the United States in the direction of a constellation in which the United States was no longer able to assert its interests against Japan and Germany, as it had done up to this point. If one were to begin such an empirical investigation today, a monopoly would be reallotted to the United States, insofar as Germany has lost its strong currency, and its social system is on the verge of collapse. Furthermore, Japan has faltered because it caught a deflationary bacillus through misguided economic policies, and has imposed a mountain of debt on its national economy, which takes away the elbow-room needed for maneuverability.

Strong economy

Hasn't the European Union taken Germany's place after the introduction of the euro? The accumulation of national populations and social products in the present and the future Union is, of course, not a basis for an international development of power as long as the core states – Germany, France, and Italy – still have ahead of them the modernization process associated with the introduction of the euro. On this point, Habermas's position is unclear. He speaks of the fact that the European welfare regimes had been exemplary for a long time, but today they are on the defensive. However, future policies aimed at the taming of capitalism must not relapse behind the yardsticks of social justice that they have established.

In a Straitjacket

The economist has a hard time with a form of argumentation that treats the 'isms' as entities that need to be tamed. But even Habermas would agree that social systems that finance themselves from payroll taxes can only survive if the number of jobs increases, rather than decreases, as the population becomes older. The functional imperatives of a common economic and currency zone have not promoted reform, as Habermas supposes. At present, the common currency is perceptible as a fiscal straitjacket, insofar as participating countries did not reduce their national debt burden before the founding of the currency union, nor did they reform their social welfare systems. They also did not make use of good economic times to take care of this. Now the stability pact forces them to clean up their budgets during economic hard times.

Currently, France and Germany are so preoccupied with their economic and socio-political reforms that they lack the economic capability, the political will, and the international respect that are necessary in order to play the role of a counter-hegemon or even to lead an EU that is willing to cede the economic high ground. This also raises the Achilles' heel of the European political mission: the answer to the question 'What is Europe?' is the central problem. Habermas's normative pronouncements show this: 'The population must so to speak "build up" their national identities, and add to them a European dimension. ... The citizens of one nation must regard the citizens of another nation as fundamentally "one of us."' The reality looks different. Habermas himself concedes this: 'Moreover, Europe is composed of nation-states that delimit one another polemically.' The most recent development has provided an illustrative example.

Yet, Habermas will not be frightened away by this. One might interpret him in this way: The EU has up till now achieved some essential things; for example, a form of governance beyond the national state. Together with its cultural achievements and historical experiences, the EU can summon the strength and discipline to form a Europe that could act as a counter-hegemon. Habermas bets on the locomotive of an *avant-garde* core Europe. With this he articulates the strategy of a 'two-speed Europe.' He sees the danger of the locomotive driving on ahead while the wagons remain standing in the station. Yet how about the locomotive itself?

'Core Europe' is generally understood as the founding states of the European Economic Community: that is, the Benelux countries, Italy, France, and Germany. But now Italy and the Netherlands have taken the side of the United States in the Iraq war; the Italian foreign minister even vehemently warned of an alliance against the United States, because this would split Europe. In principle, core Europe is reduced to the French–German tandem.

This tandem was able to drag the other member-states along with it as long as the aim was called the 'deepening of European integration,' and as long as all member-states saw in this some advantage for themselves, even a financial advantage. For

Habermas, however, it is not a question of reforms of common agricultural policy but about a foreign-policy position and a political-security position that is intended to counterbalance the power of the United States. Then, the European states would have to take a position against the United States, should the occasion arise. Such willingness is not to be expected, not now nor in the future. Many member-states see their interests more protected by the United States than by France and Germany.

The EU should focus its strengths on the requirements for integration – integration of net recipients into the European system of sectional and regional redistribution, and management of a common currency in an economic region that is itself becoming a heterogeneous economic area. If these burdens from old Europe are lifted, then respect and influence will grow automatically. And in the United States, the realization will finally dawn that even a hegemonic power can get entangled in growing difficulties when it thinks it is able to act without partners.

Frankfurter Allgemeine Zeitung, June 24, 2003

---

[1] See Jürgen Habermas. 'Warum braucht Europa eine Verfassung?' ('Why does Europe Need a Constitution?') in *Die Zeit*, no. 27, 2001. For an English translation see Jürgen Habermas, *Time of Transitions: Political Essays* (Cambridge: Polity Press, 2005).

LET THE UNITED STATES BE STRONG! EUROPE REMAINS A MID-SIZE POWER:

A Response to Jürgen Habermas

Hans-Ulrich Wehler

Jürgen Habermas's plea for Europe's 'renewal' must first withstand a careful consideration of its benefits and costs. Three of Habermas's arguments immediately make sense: first of all, the 'core Europe' of the former EC and now of the EU must be strengthened and assume an '*avant-garde*' role. This amounts to a two-speed Europe whose attraction, emanating from its dynamic center, is perhaps rightfully considered irresistible. This idea, in short, corresponds to the political plan that Wolfgang Schäuble and Karl Lamers devised for Europe ten years ago.[1] It is worth noting Habermas's reference to this correspondence in light of the inevitably approaching Grand Coalition.

Second: Europe's sense of identity must be strengthened. Unifying traditions and experiences now need to be mobilized so that the political unity of Europe can be achieved. And third: A Europe growing together politically can also pursue an independent course in its foreign and security policy. This would actively support adherence to the law of nations and a balance of power that seeks to tame the dangerous unilateralism of the United States.

It seems that arguments such as this can find a consensus. Yet the prominence of the plea also provokes objections since it highlights some unsolved or downplayed problems. Three of them shall be elaborated here: Where should Europe's borders be in the future? History cannot come to a halt with 'core Europe.' But should Europe in the near future reach even beyond the current borders of an expanded EU? Pacifism is never going to be a sufficient, durable resource of legitimacy. And finally: Europe may risk only very limited conflicts and by no means a permanently antagonistic relationship with the sole world power of the foreseeable future.

In Jürgen Habermas's plea, however, Europe's borders remain unclear. There are no problems in the north and in the west. In the south, the border facing the Arab states from Maghreb to the Near East has not, so far, been seriously questioned. In the east and southeast, however, the EU, after decades of shirking its duties, must finally make up its mind and define its border. So far cowardice has prevented politicians from asking 'emancipated citizens' to openly discuss Europe's borders and the dilemma of including new states that may be incompatible with Europe. White Russia, the Ukraine (which has already introduced a parliamentary and governmental resolution to join the EU by 2011), Moldova, Russia itself, and Turkey in particular have never been part of a historic Europe. They do not live off the legacy of Judaic, Greek or Roman antiquity that is present in Europe to this day. They have not fought their way through the far-reaching separation of state and church, and have even returned, as they did after the Bolshevist or Kemalist intermezzo, to a symbiotic relationship between the two. They have not experienced any Reformation and, even more importantly, hardly any 'Enlightenment.' They have produced no European bourgeoisie, no autonomous European bourgeois cities, no European nobility, and no European peasantry. They have not participated in the greatest achievement of European political culture since the late nineteenth century: the construction of the social welfare state. Cultural divergences are deeply engraved in Europe. Orthodox Christendom still differs greatly from a Protestant and Roman Catholic Europe that also remains separated from the Islam of Turkey by an obvious cultural barrier.

It goes without saying that it is most important to cultivate a non-conflictual, close partnership with all these neighboring states. For this purpose, a diverse set of instrumental political and economic relations is sufficient. However, these states do not belong to Europe and, therefore, do not belong to the EU. Even if, here and there, a 'privileged partnership' (Heinrich August Winkler[2]) might come about – for example with Turkey – Europe should insist on its tradition and future as a distinct unity and stick to its borders even if the leaders of these countries show an understandable urge to join Europe. The frightening alternative would be a gigantic free-trade zone from the Atlantic to Vladivostok, from Lapland to the Turkish–Iraqi border. It would mean renouncing, or, more specifically, betraying the great project of Europe's political unity that is supposed to gradually emerge from the *avant-garde* preparatory work of 'core Europe.' It would imply the loss of Europe's own political agency, its own interwoven interests, its own competitive currency, and the dependability of Europe's global influence.

Only that Europe which has historically evolved and appears in the form of the current EU – probably soon complemented by some Balkan states – possesses that basis of common traditions and experiences which will enable it to strengthen its common-European identity and put it to use for future tasks of unification after the end of the European civil wars of the twentieth century. One can exaggerate the differences between northern Finland and Sicily, between Slovenians and the Irish. Yet, on the one hand, we are dealing here with small minorities within an alliance of 450 million Europeans. On the other hand, however, one might wonder whether in 1871 there were any fewer differences between Masurian and lower Bavarian peasants, and between blue-collar workers in Hamburg and Württembergian vintners. Neither language nor religion, neither a living tradition nor a common political culture then bound together the new Germans of the Reich. Or were the differences fewer in the Italy of 1861? In this exceedingly heterogeneous, new nation-state, only 2.5 percent of the population spoke modern Italian, whereas otherwise it was generally separated by foreign dialects and various traditions that continue to live on in the North–South divide to this day. Linguistic and cultural homogenization were created in both countries only through the state's educational system. Even European politics need that kind of advance in trust which Bismarck, who was quite familiar with the great variety of German traditions, expressed when he stated that Germany would have to be put into the saddle first; after that, it would gradually learn how to ride on its own.

Europe's historical identity is a product of the aforementioned particularities, and it would be even more pronounced if its borders were finally defined and were to be defended against their constant displacement. Additionally, differences and contrasts generally promote the formation of identity. Undeniably, the Soviet threat to Europe until 1989 was a powerful motor for European politics of unification. Keeping distance, without animosity and arrogance towards non-European countries, fostered a European sense of commonality through the experience of contrast. This process was supposed to be supported by European politics without militant conflicts. That this was a Machiavellian argument, aimed at Europe's self-consolidation, was an obvious reproach that probably could have been dealt with because of the priority of European objectives.

Powerful traditions and rules of political cleverness eventually led towards Europe's legacy as the basis of its sense of identity. Pacifism, on the other hand, does not prove sufficient as an intellectual basis – not in the short run, and certainly not in the long run. The feeble desire for noble feelings leads far too quickly to their disappearance. Moreover, they are frequently tied to a moralistic feeling of superiority, as was irritatingly perceptible during the protests against the second Iraq war. One can hardly speak of the birth of a collective European public from the spirit of a noble will for peace. But were a collective European public nevertheless to come into being, it would be based on the extremely fragile foundation of a mood that cannot be sustained in the long run. Apart from serious domestic problems of integration, European interest-politics must in the future always reckon with the use of diplomatic, economic, and military means – that is, with armed intervention, whether in Macedonia or Georgia, in the Congo or any other place, as the globe is gradually condensed into a single field of action. On a domestic level as well as in foreign policy, pacifism cannot provide a durable foundation. Consistent permanent protests, stemming from a sense of pacifism – even in the case of Srebrenica? – paralyzed the EU to the point of insignificance. As a source of legitimacy, pacifism serves at best as an ornament of ad hoc decisions.

Above all, however, Europe's political unification cannot be the result of a permanent conflict with the United States. For some time to come the latter will remain the only world power, until China and perhaps India become regional hegemonic powers and until Russia has recovered. The Europeans are, fortunately, closely connected to the US through tradition and origin, language and culture, values and political institutions. It is therefore unbelievably shortsighted to count on a semi-authoritarian system like Russia's, or on a fading state communism in China, as partners against the United States.

As a reminder: during the decisive stage of the 2000 US presidential election, a tiny number of votes gave George W. Bush a victory in Florida and thus in the Electoral College. Gore safely led in the popular vote in any case. With the victory of the Republicans, the reins were taken over by a strategic clique that is power-hungry, excessively self-confident and filled with an American feeling of superiority and a religious notion of mission. It does not represent the United States *per se*. If one hypothetically imagines Washington without six key figures – Bush, Cheney, Rumsfeld, Rice, Wolfowitz, and Ashcroft – then one very much wonders, even leaving aside any conspiracy theory, whether the second Iraq war would have been prepared and carried out with such determination.

Even had Gore become president, military action after September 11 against the Taliban regime as the base camp for

Al Qaida would probably have been unavoidable, but not the war against Iraq that was planned immediately afterwards. Gore, in fact, would have kept the experienced and predominantly European-friendly teams of advisers from Ivy League universities and other intellectual strongholds of the East Coast who would not have supported such blatant unilateralism. At present it does not look as though one of the seven dwarfs of the 2004 Democratic pool of presidential candidates will be in a position to avert Bush's second term of office. Only in 2008 will the possibility for a change in government open up with Hillary Clinton. The United States would then show a different face again. In that case, should Europe's recommended course of confrontation be maintained even then, based on the ruins of past relations?

Even the new Europe, with a population of 450 million, will for a long time still remain limited to the status of a mid-sized power. Yet, according to the political convictions of my generation, it can and should finally develop into a protagonist capable of acting on an international stage. This, of course, can only happen under the condition of cooperation with a global hegemonic power, a cooperation that is close but also time and again ready for conflict. Europe cannot achieve its future by naively distancing itself from this global hegemonic power. Instead, it should stubbornly hold on to the pursuit of its own proper interests, and should not shy away from occasional harsh disputes. The basis of Europe's foreign policy in its relation to the United States should, therefore, consist of a willingness to cooperate and, at the same time, to protest energetically. Whenever the United States commits such far-reaching errors as it is doing at present, Europe would have to advise against it beforehand, urgently and privately. If Washington insists on its course of action, Europe would have to keep its distance, without losing its dignity, and for once would have to accept without malice the erroneous decisions of the hegemonic power. Of course, this demanding policy requires more than the convenient exploitation of an ill-fated anti-Americanism on the part of some European governments.

The governmental artists in Berlin immediately come to mind. Only given the priority of domestic policy, with his focus fixed on re-election, did Schröder's intense criticism of the United States win him votes, obviously without providing any damage control through confidential talks with Washington. This proven recipe was later the basis for election campaigns in Hessen and Lower Saxony, yet it remained ineffective. A European form of criticism of Washington's belligerence was of paramount importance at the time. Such failed and incompetent political strategy, and intermittently rising sentiments of pacifism, cannot serve as the basis for a future Europe policy.

European independence and European self-confidence, however, could certainly develop further in strategically limited conflicts with the United States. If, on the other hand, Europe were to make this conflict with the United States permanent, then it could – since its development into an independent actor is so excruciatingly slow (best example: its military force) – end up on the losing side and consequently find itself in an extremely dangerous entanglement with its Russian and Chinese allies. On a marginal note: A country which usually sells just about 7 percent of its gross national product outside the Western hemisphere is much less vulnerable than a European economy that would not be in a position to retaliate if the United States were to complicate trade relations.

What has made the integration of Europe possible during the past half-century, if not the protective screen provided by the United States and its various forms of political support? Has everything been forgotten, not to mention the United States' unique support of the German unification process, in the fervor of the election campaign? And only because the clique around Bush has massively exploited the special constellation that came into being after September 11, supported by a belligerently exalted 'patriotism,' as American missionary nationalism is often euphemistically called? With whom does one agree more readily than with the numerous American critics in their polemics against belligerence and unilateralism? Should this country, whose scrupulous self-scrutiny and astonishing regeneration so far could always be counted on, be determined solely by the militancy of the Bush government and those segments of the electorate and the public that support it?

Is it really that difficult, now that anti-American pacifism is fading away, to let practical politics be guided again by sober insight into a permanent constellation of interests that connect Europe, and here especially Germany, with the United States? Europe will remain dependent on a close collaboration with Washington for some time to come, and its economic and political potential should not fuel conceit. Looking for allegedly superior partners someplace else can only end in a fiasco.

Frankfurter Allgemeine Zeitung, June 27, 2003

---

[1] Karl Lamers, foreign policy expert for the German Christian Democratic Union, and Wolfgang Schäuble, former Party Chairman, published their highly influential position paper introducing the notion of 'core Europe' in 1994. For a version of their position in English, see Karl Lamers and Wolfgang Schäuble, 'Reflections on European Policy,' in Brent Nelson and Alexander Stubb, eds, *The European Union: Readings on the Theory and Practice of European Integration*, 3rd edition (London: Palgrave Macmillan, 2003).

[2] Hans August Winkler is a leading German historian and influential member of the Social Democratic Party.

PLEASE DON'T BE SO SENSITIVE:

Jürgen Habermas Continues Arguing
for Europe in Berlin

Gustav Seibt

The idea of the nation was born in tiny debating circles of
students and professors – particularly in those two 'delayed'
nations whose formation was the product of a voluntary political act preceded by a long process of cultural development:
Germany and Italy. Pipe-smoking fraternity members and fiery
armchair orators, newspaper readers, coffee-house goers and
opera patrons, together created the kind of abstract idea which
encompassed all social classes and abolished all social and
regional differences, and which seems so normal to us today:
the fatherland with its promise of social participation for all
its citizens.

The debate about a European identity that Jürgen Habermas
and his fellow supporters initiated in the big newspapers of
Western Europe, among others the *Süddeutsche Zeitung*, on the
last weekend of May is remarkably similar to the embryonic
situation of *Risorgimento* nationalism in the early nineteenth
century. We are witnessing a thoroughly academic discussion,
that is to say, a discussion that is as fiery as it is abstractly idealistic, and that refers to two current experiences of this spring:
the disputes among European governments in light of the
unilateral American effort in the Iraq war on the one hand,
and the wave of pacifism sweeping through populations across
Europe on the other.

Jürgen Habermas, the philosopher of communicative action,
wishes to dramatize this conflict intellectually and turn it into

the birthday of a European public opinion. The success is astonishing. That this public, which is now mobilized all across Europe, currently consists only of polyglot readers of sophisticated papers, of educated classes and literati far from the ordinary democratic masses, is no objection to a campaign that refers to a historical model with such consistency.

An Audience of Citizens

Articles must turn into meetings, lectures into programs and actions; this would be the old European way. There was another scene of this idealistic stage production on Friday evening in Berlin, in a widely attended panel discussion organized by Adolf Muschg, the new president of the *Akademie der Künste* (Academy of Arts) and Swiss fellow-supporter of the Habermas campaign. It is an exalting sight when, of a clear evening, hundreds of people run not to their barbecues after their workdays but into the gloomy halls of Werner Düttmann's austere academy building; when, in other words, the gregarious crowd forms into an 'audience of citizens,' as Habermas put it during his opening speech. And for whomever a tear of emotion briefly veiled the eye, the scenery might have appeared like a metal engraving from an old book.

On the platform next to Habermas and Muschg were the Polish philosopher Zdzislaw Krasnodebski, the constitutional lawyer Jutta Limbach, and the CDU politician Wolfgang Schäuble, who in 1994 had invented the keyword with the idea of a 'core Europe,' which Habermas has now made the focal point of the discussion. The audience, animated partly by a historically grounded ideology, had the opportunity to appreciate how Habermas, in full approval, quoted long passages from a resolution of the CDU, which concerned foreign policy and demanded a greater legal codification of international relations. And the audience was equally happy when Schäuble, firmly agreeing with Habermas, again took up his idea of a core Europe, which should not promote division but help make Europe more dynamic – in order to make possible a two-speed

Europe, that is, an inner-European *avant-garde*. The latter fully corresponds to Habermas's idea that an internationally united core Europe consisting of France, Germany and the Benelux states would soon have the effect of an irresistible attraction on the remaining countries.

Why is Habermas suddenly so interested in foreign policy? It is not only the depressing experience of European weakness in the dispute over international law with the United States that accounts for his interest; there is a much more important point as well. The EU, according to Habermas, must grow beyond the functional integration of an economic community and acquire the qualities of a state. For this to happen, however, an ongoing 'normative integration' would be necessary, that is, a reference to shared values in a public realm extending beyond the borders of individual countries. Only such a normative integration would transform European citizens into fellow-citizens living side by side, so that a Finn and a Portuguese could feel and share the solidarity of a common destiny. That, in turn, is for Habermas not only the precondition but also the effect of a successful European foreign policy.

'For the promotion of such a European identity a symbolically-charged foreign and security policy offers itself,' states Habermas, 'the themes of which enjoy particular prominence, especially today, with the threat of international terrorism and the highly controversial answer of the American government to this challenge.' In the language of classical international relations, one could say the following: Europe's international standing is supposed to promote Europe's process of self-discovery. That, however, can only happen through the essentially moral competition with the United States that Habermas demanded at the beginning of his campaign – under keywords such as technological scepticism, secularization, welfare state, and multilateralism.

The Polish author Zdzislaw Krasnodebski entered the debate as a representative of those nations that, in the context of conceptions such as this, occupy a marginal rather than a central

position. In a notably lamenting tone, his counter-argument
noted the German press's disdainful comments about the Polish
role in the Iraq war ('the little victor') and the one-sidedness
of Habermas's identity categories – as democracy and religion
belong together in Poland just as much as freedom and dereg-
ulation – which contradicts Eastern European experiences so
flagrantly. For Poles, after the events of the Pershing period in
1982, there is nothing delightful about Western European peace
demonstrations; yet a general lack of curiosity about the
Solidarity movement was, after all, also an essential characteristic of Western pacifism.

For Poland, an overcoming of the division within Europe
takes priority over Europe's potential role as a counterforce to
the United States. Krasnodebski interprets the intention behind
the supposedly anti-hegemonic notion of a core Europe as
hegemonic itself – on the European stage. Poland did not join
Europe in order to make sure 'that Peter Struck[1] would come
face to face with Donald Rumsfeld,' he stated poignantly. Jutta
Limbach, too, could not believe in the pioneering role of a
core Europe, noting that the time for this was already over: in
the present the idea has a discriminating effect and, in the final
instance, plays into the hands of the United States. The idea
of an 'effect of attraction' would apply to economic rather than
to foreign relations; in the power struggle between states, cores
usually repel rather than attract one another, provoking action
from other cores. Schäuble therefore warned against an 'anti-
American definition' of European identity, insisting on the
commonality of European and American security interests.

We should not let Europe fail precisely because the European
attempt has shown that it is 'effective on a cosmopolitan level,'
explained Adolf Muschg. He referred to the impressive demonstration of solidarity through European transfer payments that
protected entire countries from global market dumping. That
Poland wishes to participate in that kind of solidarity, rather
than in the restoration of a Trianon Europe,[2] is only natural.
Habermas, with passionate vigor, in the end defended himself

against the charge of anti-Americanism, which he can only find 'silly' and 'ridiculous,' because what is at stake for him in the invocation of American principles is merely an opposition against current American policy. Moreover, identity inevitably expresses itself in relation to the closest Other.

He considered the Polish objections plausible; however, he also conceded them merely the rank of 'sensitivities.' Furthermore, anything, including each European particularity, will take on a different appearance under a microscope. Habermas prefers the telescope; his apparently quite German élan with the production of ideas has something impatient about it, since deviating historical experiences count for little in light of those higher principles that are so essential for him. Europe, however, remains tough, fragmented, and full of peculiarities. Finally, Wolfgang Schäuble uttered perhaps one of the most thoughtful sentences of this lively discussion: 'If we become solely Europeans, we will destroy Europe.'

Süddeutsche Zeitung, June 29, 2003

---

[1] Peter Struck is Germany's defence minister under the SPD–Green coalition government.

[2] The 1920 Treaty of Trianon effectively divided most of Hungary's pre-First World War territory amongst the allied powers.

AT THE FLEA MARKET:

Europe's Refusal to be Defined by Its Antiques

Johannes Willms

It has not been too long since one question in particular occupied the minds of this country: What is German, and what is Germany? The question concerning the essence of German identity has been struggled over with the hallowed sense of seriousness that has always characterized German intellectuals. As is well known, the answer did not spring from Minerva's brow. Rather, it was provided by the self-dissolution of the Eastern bloc, an event which realized the chance for a peaceful unification of the two German states, embedded within the framework of a greater European order.

We are now embroiled in a new identity debate, one that is at least as sterile as the earlier one and which, characteristically, takes place mostly in Germany, although it allegedly does not concern us alone. It concerns the fateful question of what Europe is supposed to be, and, in turn, who is supposed to belong to it. Nothing less than the unity of Europe depends on the resolution of this question. However, European unity is inconceivable without a prior determination of a foundation that is meaningful to everyone, representing a consensus on common and basic European values. 'Europe's sense of identity,' as Hans Ulrich Wehler recently proclaimed *ex cathedra*, 'must be strengthened. Unifying traditions and experiences now need to be mobilized so that the political unity of Europe can be achieved.' (*Frankfurter Allgemeine Zeitung*, June 27, 2003.)

As a historian, Wehler should know that the conjuring or even mobilizing of so-called 'unifying traditions and experiences' of European nations has its own dynamic, which may either lead to failure or become politically effective only by way of a fatal production of ideology. The main reason for this is that the historical nature of Europe cannot be tied to a specific sense of identity that all European states, with their common experience, could share. Europe's countries have certainly some elements in common. However, these elements are neither so unambiguous nor equally constitutive for the respective cultural and political consciousness of individual nations that they could be used as components for the formation of an overarching sense of identity.

Questionable Arbitrariness

The European identity that Wehler declares indispensable, in particular, is supposed to provide demarcations and exclusions, and furnish the criteria for determining who might claim to belong to Europe, and who has to remain excluded from it forever. As a result of the lack of 'natural' boundaries demarcating Europe in the east and southeast, a European sense of identity is supposed to assume this indispensable function. This is, according to Prof. Wehler, all the more necessary to the degree that 'cowardice has prevented politicians from asking "emancipated citizens" to openly discuss Europe's borders and the dilemma of including new states that may be incompatible with Europe.' The latter included, according to Wehler, White Russia, the Ukraine, Moldova, Russia and, 'first and foremost,' Turkey, all of which have supposedly 'never been part of a historic Europe.'

Wehler identifies this 'historic Europe' as a *Mixtum Compositum* that originated from the legacy of Judaic, Greek, and Roman antiquity, and that appears as a unity constituted by a number of unique characteristics marking its historical emergence. What Wehler does not mention, however, is that to this very day this process has by no means been concluded and is much rather characterized by considerable temporal differences and setbacks, permitting a quite different determination of borders. The arbitrariness of Wehler's criteria happens to coincide with their dubious exemplarity. Neither the Reformation, which he represented as constitutive for 'historic Europe,' nor the Enlightenment constitute historical experiences in which all nations and states supposedly belonging to Europe have equally participated. The Iberian peninsula lacks this kind of experience, just as do middle and southern Italy, Ireland, or even Greece.

The same holds true for the other positions of Wehler's criteria, whose fulfillment he uses to differentiate 'Europe-compatible countries' from all those that must remain excluded: the European bourgeoisie, the autonomous European bourgeois cities, the European nobility, or even the European peasantry. All of these are socio-historical phenomena that, in the individual countries of 'historic Europe,' showed highly distinct forms, whose significance for each country's political development has to be clearly differentiated. Autonomous bourgeois cities – that is, cities that were not integrated into the confederacy of states – existed at the most in the German empire and in Italy, whereas the European nobility had always leapt over the imaginary boundaries of 'historic Europe' through marriage. And, from a historical perspective, a peasantry that cultivated its holdings as landowners existed neither in Spain nor east of the Elbe.

This clearly shows that 'historic Europe,' which Wehler seeks to establish as a distinct particularity, is characterized by profound contradictions and significant temporal differences that cannot be explained from an objective historical perspective, but rather ideologically at best. If one wanted to find a common historical ground for the Europe that Wehler envisions, then it would be the Europe in which the Crusade mania dominated political reality. However, a Europe that would identify its future essence with such a dubious historical model would be doomed to failure as a completely anachronistic monster.

The European diplomats in Maastricht who pointed the way toward Europe's eastward expansion were certainly no cowards; they were actually quite intelligent in not imposing historic and cultural limitations on this project. By not doing so, they implicitly displayed their determination to politically and culturally shape the pan-European space that opened up after the end of the Cold War. This perspective may disturb quite a few people, and to maintain it will predictably create many problems. Yet, at the same time, it is the only position that can be justified as politically wise.

Süddeutsche Zeitung, July 1, 2003

EUROPE HAS TO EUROPEANIZE ITSELF:

The Pothole

Mathias Greffrath

> *'Europe might just save the world.'*
> – Richard Rorty

If we really were the Europe that Habermas, Rorty, and others dream about, we would already have the first candidate for exit: Italy. As matters stand, Berlusconi is only an extremely talented representative of the really existing Western community of values. Kohl, too, was good at the corrupt combination of mass media and politics; the United States is the leader when it comes to imposing conformity; Elf wasn't the first scandal of state monopolies in Paris; and Blair's suggestion of incarcerating refugees is a weak version of the 'cannon-against-boatpeople' populism *à la* Bossi. The outrage about the Godfather will subside after a few weeks of discussion in the newspapers, because Berlusconi faithfully adheres to the global constitution: the Washington consensus. As long as the latter is in effect, with its rulings about cutbacks in the social welfare system, castration of the state, the privatization raids, and a global reserve army, all responses by Europe and its empire, as they circulate in newspapers, are without substance.

No, I have nothing against the initiative of intellectuals to bestow global utility on the values of old Europe, whether it is universalism, international law, the social welfare state, or indeed, statehood in general. It's just that it comes too late. A generation too late, as it happens, since the path to empire (the free global game of multinational concerns, capital markets, and monopoly media) was cleared two decades ago, actively tolerated by international social democrats. And ten years too late because the years after the fall of the Wall were not used to propagate the vision of a democratic and social Europe and to demand corresponding sacrifices from Western European societies. Thus, we returned to Europe, says a Romanian ex-reformer, but that Europe isn't there any more.

Back then, Jacques Delors perceived the opportunities and costs of eastward expansion, and suggested promoting it with a spectacular industrial policy: to build public transport systems connecting Helsinki, Belgrade, and Athens, Lisbon with Paris, Warsaw with Moscow. Delors foresaw that the pressures on Europe, insofar as it wanted to preserve its civilization, would demand an increased willingness for sacrifice from the consuming masses; even back then, he began to think about European community service for young people. Projects of that kind went unnoticed in the frenzy of economic settlement in the East and the push for liberalization in the West. Thus for years only a lone French sociologist by the name of Bourdieu walked across the country making strong statements like: the European welfare state is an achievement, as precious as Mozart, Kant, and Beethoven; one must defend it.

It would have been nice. The draft of the EU constitution provides neither for a European right to work, nor for any effective protection from the commercialization of the educational and health systems and of the public sector in general. And citizens of this Europe are supposed to save the world, as Richard Rorty implores? Where is this idealism that European public opinion is to force on its politicians supposed to come from?

The difficulty that Habermas and Derrida foresee, the development of an inspiring vision for Europe, lies precisely in the fact that the frontline position of the United States does not reach far enough. A social Europe is not only feared by American billionaires but by the executives at Allianz, Daimler, and Siemens who no longer pay taxes, as well as by their stock-holders, and by the liberal European elites. Already today, you need to shout a little louder to bring the European project to the attention of the European people, especially young Europeans, as was demanded during the Nice summit. After all, more and more people in core Europe, especially the young ones, experience Europe as a deterioration of their standard of living.

Anyone still babbling about Europe today, as Jan Ross once scornfully put it in the German newspaper *Die Zeit*, is desperately grasping for the last available slogan for the European left after it bid farewell to socialism. We'd have a better chance of finding and studying the new Europe in Poland, in the Baltic States, and in Romania. There, the primacy of freedom and the hope for innovation have supposedly found a home – a highly imaginative circumscription of the deregulated wild world, and a nice testimony to the successfully functioning class instinct of educated high society.

For what makes the Turkish, the Romanians, and the Moroccans come to Europe? An empire that has reconciled capitalism and communism. Their arrival is threatening, and the alternative is not any less costly: a strong Europe whose survival depends on a front yard filled with weapons, an endlessly expanding economy, and an irresistible drive toward democratization.

Yet even that alternative is threatening: to Western European landowners with no need for Polish vegetables; to the new millionaires in Romania who want the liberalism but not the social constitution of Western Europe; for the German middle class that benefits disproportionately from the welfare state; for the big corporations whose freedom of action would be reduced under a European-wide taxation and social policy; above all, however, for the lower classes in rich Euro-countries whose living standards even today still rely on the fact that the shirts they purchase at H&M are sewn in Transylvania for fifty cents an hour, and that tomatoes are so cheap because there are no labor laws in Morocco. How would they benefit from a Greater Europe?

In the short term, there would be no benefit. But if the statistics are correct, more and more European citizens feel that the dynamic of globalization also affects them. It would be the task of the Social Democrats to connect the victims of the present with the vision of a Europe strong and geographically large enough to counteract the force of financial markets and of the plutocratic United States of America. For that to happen, however, they would have to consider more seriously the untimely thoughts that a world economy without any limits (as Adam Smith already said) leads to collective misery, that there is no modern democracy without the protection of collective goods, and that a world community of democracies is not possible without a re-regionalization of the world economy and the democratization of the really-existing world governments, the IMF, the WTO, and the OECD. For this, however, we would need a Europe that speaks with one voice, and that voice has to be social-democratic. The misery of the Social Democratic Party of Germany lies in the fact that half of its members in the Bundestag believe this as well, while its leadership does not.

If there is indeed something to be criticized about Habermas, it is the timidity with which he hides in an inconspicuous paragraph the battles that we are about to face for the restructuring of the world economic organizations instead of, let us say it boldly, making a point of becoming a new member of *Attac,* a group whose strategists are not even considering abandoning democratic socialism, however difficult that may be. In the short term, they count on the EU citizens' right to plebiscite that is guaranteed in the EU constitution, a right, of course, that is going to perish in the streets if unions and leftist parties do not Europeanize *a tempo.*

Die Tageszeitung, July 2, 2003

THE RENEWAL OF EUROPE:

Response to Habermas

Timothy Garton Ash and Ralf Dahrendorf

One might think that we are experiencing a renaissance of Gaullism – though with two slight differences. This time around, it is not about the glory of France but that of 'core Europe.' Also, it is not so much the political leaders but rather the intellectuals who speak out for a European identity that defines itself in its contrast to the United States. Jürgen Habermas and Jacques Derrida, however, agree with de Gaulle insofar as they find the encouragement for their project on the streets – in a kind of *volonté générale* of the anti-war and anti-Bush demonstrations in the European capitals on February 15, 2003.

In their arguments, the two philosophers refer to a colleague of equal rank, namely Immanuel Kant. They think, as Derrida opines in his introduction, 'according to the spirit, if not the precise sense, that refers back to the Kantian tradition.' And Habermas concludes his text with the 'Kantian hope for a world domestic policy.' This is also a response to the American neo-conservative Robert Kagan, who wishes to crown Kant as the philosopher-king of the EU in his polemic about the power of the United States and Europe's impotence.

Kant did not think much of philosopher-kings – 'because the possession of power inevitably spoils the free exercise of reason' – but as the pioneer thinker of a European union, he definitely has his place. Yes, we are Kantians! Yet in the mutually reinforcing Kant-portraits of Habermas and Kagan, namely those of the intellectual Euro-Gaullist and of the American neo-conservative, each of which reinforces the other, we barely recognize the great thinker of the Enlightenment anymore. 'The Europeans,' writes Kagan, 'have stepped out from the Hobbesian world of anarchy into the Kantian world of perpetual peace.' The philosopher from Königsberg could not possibly have anticipated that someone would ever interpret his essay title 'Perpetual Peace' (namely in the cemetery) in this way – a title, by the way, which he ironically borrowed from a Dutch pub sign.

No, both authors confuse Kant with Rousseau. Immanuel Kant was carved from an altogether different, harder wood than the Genevan dreamer of Arcadias. Not only did Kant know that power exists, but he thanked nature 'for cantankerousness, for jealous vanity always seeking competition, for the insatiable desire to possess and even to rule.' Only through the 'unsociable sociability' of people, that is, through multiplicity and fission, through 'antagonism,' can people escape from the Arcadian idyll, in which 'in a condition of absolute harmony, frugality and mutual love, all talent would forever wither in the bud.'

With Cosmopolitan Intent

We are Kantians. Like Kant, we wish for a bourgeois – and ultimately cosmopolitan – society, which universally administers the law, and which is forever imperfect and full of conflict, but, above all, open. A renewed Europe can contribute to it a great deal, just as the United States has done for more than 200 years again and again.

This will, however, be a Europe that has features different from those which Habermas ascribes to the European present and future. His image of Europe reminds one at times of West Germany before the end of an epoch in 1989. Certainly, 'the experiences of totalitarian regimes of the twentieth century' and also the 'bellicose past' connect perpetrators and victims. But is religion indeed anywhere in Europe so apolitical?

In Ireland? In Poland? In England, where even the parliament publicly prays before taking up its official business? And the 'emancipation of civil society from the tutelage of an absolutistic regime' was equally not a British, Italian, or Swiss phenomenon.

The renewal of Europe is necessary. But this will never be accomplished by an endeavored self-determination of Europe as un- or even anti-American. Each attempt to define Europe vis-à-vis the United States will not unify Europe but divide it. The history of the Iraq crisis has shown this all too clearly. Habermas interprets the demonstrations of February 15 as a unanimous response of the European peoples to 'those declarations of loyalty towards Bush' which eight heads of government and state, led by José María Aznar and Tony Blair, had declared shortly beforehand. This interpretation is misleading in three respects: firstly, because the demonstrations were in fact not a reaction to the 'letter of the eight'; secondly, because that letter – signed by statesmen who are known for their obsequiousness, such as Václav Havel – was more a recognition of Western values and transatlantic relations than a recognition of George W. Bush; and thirdly, because the letter was born as a reaction to the French–German unilateral effort against a second UN resolution. Thus, this venture of an '*avant-garde* core Europe' did not unite Europe but divided it.

No, the driving force behind a European renewal has to be that kind of applied enlightenment that connects Europe and the United States – and that wins over more people and countries in the world through success and persuasiveness. The Kantian hope for a world domestic policy is the positive side of globalization. In this regard, specifically European approaches and achievements indeed need to be carefully considered. They might also serve as a role model. We will name only a few.

On May 1, 2004, the European Union will encompass twenty-five nations. Fifteen long, perhaps too long, years after the first cut through the Iron Curtain, a dream comes true. The clear majority of European nations, which for centuries had fought bloody wars against each other, will for the first time – and endowed with equal rights – belong to one and the same peaceful political and economic community. There has never been anything like this in Europe. No other continent can offer anything of this nature. Should we not, therefore, declare the European birthday to be May 1, which unites us, rather than February 15, which divides us?

Another important European approach is linked to future expansion; that is, political criteria for potential members determined by the European Council in Copenhagen in 1993. These 'Copenhagen Criteria' demand, above all, stable democratic institutions, the rule of law, respect for human rights, and the protection of minorities. In addition, there are regulations concerning the market economy, including the independence of the Central Bank. With this, the EU has become, far beyond the founding treaties, a model for the constitution of freedom, the acceptance of which it consistently demands from its potential members.

'European welfare states,' as Habermas writes, 'were also for a long time role models.' As a matter of fact, there were always great differences between countries that can afford an expensive welfare state and those that cannot afford it; today, one would have to include most of the Central and Eastern European member-states among the latter. Furthermore, New Zealand and Canada (and some states of the USA) are closer to the 'European social model' than some European nations. It is correct, however, that Europe has developed a rich variety of more or less well-functioning forms of democratic capitalism. They all have in common that they seek to complete the core task as it was formulated by Adair Turner: 'to combine a dynamic economy and the liberating effect of economic independence with the goal of creating an all-inclusive society, in light of the fact that free markets alone cannot achieve this.'

In the end, such approaches lead once more back to Kant. It is the 'cosmopolitan intent' to act in such a way that our actions can be thought of as a principle of a cosmopolitan society universally administering the law. The road to the achievement of this goal may seem far, in fact the goal may seem unattainable in its abundance, but it directs what we do and what we do not do. Not every version of the European Union advocated today and not every government in Washington has obeyed such maxims. They do, however, describe the Europe and the United States that we want and, thus, their common purpose.

Süddeutsche Zeitung, July 5, 2003

Shouldn't why europe is caring together be more firmly est. before an effort to link everyone in

Still trying to Find EU commonality while holding onto nationalism a constitutional is made?

FIRST KANT, NOW HABERMAS:

A Polish Perspective on 'Core Europe'

Adam Krzeminski

Since Jürgen Habermas and other Western European intellectuals took a stand against the United States by promoting the pacifist, so-called 'old' core Europe to the status of a European '*avant-garde*' (*Neue Zürcher Zeitung*, May 31, 2003), there has been no end to critical responses. A particularly attentive reaction has come from Poland, which belongs to the 'new' Europe.

The so-called 'younger' Europe of the East appeared only slightly more than one thousand years ago in the history of European civilization and, since the Enlightenment, has either been effaced from Western consciousness or degraded to the status of material at the disposal of European empires. It is only now confirming its will through referenda to join the Carolingian Europe that had held it in check by force for half a century. The consequence of the Yalta agreement was that Western Europe could live safely under American protection, whereas East–Central Europeans were subjugated to the Soviet-Russian dictatorship.

The moral legitimization of the current membership is, of course, the 'velvet revolution,' an event whose foundations were laid by the politics of *détente* of the 1970s and Reagan's strategy of confrontation, by Gorbachev's *Perestroika* from above and the pressure from below by civil rights campaigners. Here in the East – in Warsaw, Budapest, Prague, Leipzig, and Vilnius – the winds of historical change blew more strongly than in Paris, Frankfurt, Zurich, or Madrid. No one in the West rejoiced after the East-Central European 'Autumn of the People.' In Paris or London there was actually a great deal of embarrassed discontent arising from German unification and the feared influx of the poor to the West. Even fourteen years later, there is obviously no feeling of joy within 'core Europe' over the EU's eastward expansion. On the 'Euro-barometer,' the level of agreement is dropping as quickly in France, Germany, or Austria as it is increasing in the new member countries.

Whereas the US was organized democratically from the very beginning, Europe seems to maintain its feudal framework. Over centuries, it had been built according to the principle of seniority. And even now, frightened that the barbarians have captured the outer walls of the EU after all, the economic and spiritual warriors of the Occident are attempting to retreat into the redoubt of 'core Europe,' probably in the hope that hosts of angels will provide for relief. Politically, they wish to remain among themselves as '*avant-garde*'; economically, they think of tightening the Maastricht criteria for the euro-zone so that none of the poor can intrude. And finally, the latter are also deliberately excluded from a philosophical dispute concerning Europe's spirit. Jürgen Habermas forgives the Spaniards and Italians their American infidelity because they have always been part of the West; yet, he does not forgive the Polish and Hungarians. They never belonged to Europe's inner circle, say the Lords of the Rings. They will first have to humbly wait outside, wearing the penitential robes of their poverty, until the doors are opened for them.

Sarcasm, Poignancy, Irony

In the dispute with the great minds of the West, the East-Central Europeans nowadays mostly arm themselves with sarcasm, like Péter Esterházy, or with irony, like Andrzej Stasiuk. If they wish to argue on the basis of principles, like Zdzislaw Krasnodebski, then they put on the toga of American neo-conservatives and earn catcalls. Polish reality is different. As

Catholic as the Polish might be, they act just as anti-clerically; they are far from the messianism of power as George W. Bush embodies it. At one point they vote for the left, then for the right, but most of the time they vote for the middle and ignore bigoted splinter groups. They agree with the Pope in questions concerning membership in the EU, but not in questions concerning the Iraq war, where they let themselves instead be guided by pragmatic considerations. On that particular February 15, 2003, which Habermas declared the birthday of a Western European public, a total of 4 percent of Poles supported the war, and not even 4,000 in the streets opposed it. The rest accepted it, out of solidarity with the only custodian of law in the world that is willing and able to act, as well as out of its own interests, for war is not an end in itself but a continuation of politics by other means. To leave everything as it was only for the sake of peace would merely have been a mockery of peace.

The Poles know this only too well from their own history. They also cultivate a quite different military culture than do the former colonial powers. For 150 years, from the 1795 Kosciusko Rebellion, which was directed militarily against the Russians and politically against the partitioning powers, to the 1944 Warsaw Rebellion, which was directed militarily against the Germans and politically against Stalin, military actions by Polish volunteers were a political sign: Poland still exists. This was the meaning behind those Polish legions that entered battle on the side of Napoleon in 1797 and the company of volunteers that marched under the command of Józef Pilsudski on the side of the Central Powers from Krakow towards Warsaw in 1914. It was a symbolic–romantic deed, and yet it was also politically sensible and even successful in the end. Although it was only partially successful under Napoleon because he betrayed his Polish auxiliary troops after all, it was extremely successful under Pilsudski, because four years later the Polish state existed once more after 123 years. This was, among other things, due to the fact that the Poles were not lackeys of one or the other side, but rather, with the modest possibilities of a nation that was politically 'no longer existent,' collectively weighed all available options.

Mistrust

This historical appeal is not unjustified. When Adolf Muschg extols to the 'core Europeans' the Swiss model of a voluntary fusion of Swiss citizens, it must be legitimate not only to emphasize the century-long experiences of federalism in East-Central Europe (the Polish–Lithuanian union lasted, after all, 400 years and was then hobbled, carved up, and crushed by Russia, Prussia, and Austria), but also to point out the political philosophies that have been developed in that part of Europe in the last 200 years.

Poles have good reason to mistrust the Kantian 'perpetual peace' that was cited time and again in the debate surrounding the Iraq war. As wonderful, noble, and well-intentioned as Kant's work is, to a Pole it can also appear as an expression of cowardice. It was published in October 1795 during the Leipzig Fair, exactly one month after the third partition of Poland, which meant the final liquidation of an old state by its neighboring countries, among them, notably, Prussia. Kant carefully alluded to the Polish question in the fifth preliminary article of his cosmopolitan system of peace: 'No state shall violently interfere with the constitution and government of another,' yet he could never bring himself to clearly protest against the Poland policy of Friedrich II and his successors. He was too withdrawn from the world, too immersed in his speculative patterns of thought. But not quite completely; Kant could indeed be very direct, and both the Polish state and the Polish way of life served him often, as it did to many Prussians at the time, as a deterring example of a nation without culture: 'Until just recently, the principle of barbaric freedom in Poland, until it became a mere proverb, since laws were no longer enforceable, was that the one who possessed greatest force possessed the greatest power. A people set for barbaric freedom does not voluntarily give it up. It is so sweet to them that they would rather subject themselves to other occurrences instead of doing without a continuous freedom. Such a people must be educated by force. Free nations are arrogant and lazy when free, and this freedom makes them once again arrogant. They do not feel like working because nothing forces them to do so and thus they consider those who work to be slaves,' said Kant in his 'Lectures on Anthropology.'

Only a Trifle ...

Polish authors had already expressed themselves in a similarly critical manner, and they launched a reform process. This was for Kant, unfortunately, only a trifle. In March 1792 – which means already after the reforms of the Great Sejm (1788–92),[1] the culmination of which was the first written constitution in Europe of May 3, 1791 – he wrote sceptically: 'Nothing can be inferred with confidence for the future from what happened among the Polish' ('Dohna Anthropology,' fragment of March 3, 1792). He did not write clearly and precisely, as, for example, Edmund Burke did, that a Russian intervention (with Prussian participation) was apparently a violation of the law of nations. When Poland was finally effaced after the quelled revolt, Kant wrote his draft of 'Perpetual Peace,' without, however, giving any thought to how one could make good a flagrant viola-tion of the law of nations. Nor was he convinced that Poland should be reestablished as an entity, and in 1798, in the 'The Contest of Faculties,' he wrote: 'Poland: that is a very strange country ... With them, there are no middle classes, and thus, they have little culture ... For usually, culture comes from the middle classes.' This might be very well be the case according to the German model, but is it indeed the measure of all things?

Thus Kant, too, exhibits the basic Prussian conviction that the Polish people are to blame for their own ruin. Although, in an ideal case of 'Perpetual Peace,' one may not intervene in the midst of a reform process, one may nevertheless 'educate' a 'strange country' with force. Is it thus permissible to take violent measures against barbaric freedom, but not against a barbaric despotism?

Accusing Kant of stigmatizing (the) Polish (lack of) culture would verge on the obsessive. Kant, and later Hegel, were not the last German thinkers who regarded the liquidation of the Polish–Lithuanian *res publica* as a Last Judgment for which Poland had no one to blame but itself. The sympathy with the 'brave' and 'unfortunate' Poles and the cheap pathos of the 'Polish songs' in the nineteenth century did not change anything about the fact that one could imagine Europe, at least within German-speaking culture, very well without Poland. A glance at Jacob Burckhardt's 'Observations from the Point of View of World History' confirms this. To this day, Poland appears three times in the historical consciousness of the German bourgeoisie: as an amorphous mass that was partitioned in the eighteenth century, for which it had no one to blame but itself; as a pre-modern nation's urge for freedom in the nineteenth and twentieth centuries; and as the beneficiary of the European 'original catastrophe' of the First World War, of the 'false' peace of Versailles. It was only the German invasion of Poland in 1939, the country's shifting to the west at the expense of Germany in 1945, and the Polish resistance against the Communist regime that made Poland the focus of attention not only of German intellectuals.

The deliberate non-invitation of Poles, Hungarians or Czechs to the great debate about the European spirit might have been meant as a pedagogical measure; however, it follows an old tradition. The message is unequivocal: Europe's spiritual driving forces are we, the Germans, French, Italians, Spanish, and Anglo-Saxons. All the others must first show that they deserve to belong among this group. Whether they deserve it or not, the East-Central Europeans will come. In fact, they are already here, *intra muros*. And they will also conquer the high fortress of occidental warriors, not in order to raze them to the ground, but instead to take their seats and enjoy equal rights at the Round Table of the Union.

Neue Zürcher Zeitung, July 11, 2003

---

[1] The Great or Four-Year Sejm (Diet) of 1788–92 was a sustained legislative effort to assert Poland's independence from Russia, and led to the adoption of a new Polish constitution in 1792 and, with it, the transformation of Poland into a constitutional monarchy.

DE-CENTERING THE PROJECT
OF GLOBAL DEMOCRACY

Iris Marion Young

In an important statement co-signed by Jacques Derrida and published in the *Frankfurter Allgemeine Zeitung* on May 31, 2003, Jürgen Habermas calls upon European states and citizens to forge a common European foreign policy to balance the hegemonic power of the United States. Europeans should forge a common political identity to stand up to this hegemonic power, but an identity that is open toward ideas of cosmopolitan democracy. I am grateful to these civic-minded philosophers for issuing such a call to public responsibility at this historical moment when the United States and the United Kingdom seem ready to occupy Iraq indefinitely, and the US threatens other states. I welcome the call for Europe to be more independent of the United States in assessing its own interests and the interests of the world, and I agree that a united and different stance from Europe might temper the arrogance of US foreign policy. I wonder, however, just how cosmopolitan is the stance taken in the statement. From the point of view of the rest of the world, and especially from the point of view of the states and people in the global South, the philosophers' appeal may look more like a re-centering of Europe than the invocation of an inclusive global democracy.

Habermas begins by citing February 15, 2003 as a historic day, which may 'go down in history as a sign of the birth of a European public sphere.' On that day, he notes, millions rallied to oppose war in Iraq, in cities across Europe, including London,

Rome, Madrid, Barcelona, Berlin, and Paris. It is the coordinated simultaneity of these demonstrations, Habermas suggests,
that harbingers a European public sphere.

But this interpretation distorts the historical facts. On that
same weekend there were mass demonstrations on every other
continent as well – in Sydney, Tokyo, Seoul, Manila, Vancouver,
Toronto, Mexico City, Tegucigalpa, São Paulo, Lagos,
Johannesburg, Nairobi, Tel Aviv, Cairo, Istanbul, Warsaw,
Moscow, and hundreds of other cities, including many in the
US. According to people with whom I have spoken, the worldwide coordination of these demonstrations was planned at the
third meeting of the World Social Forum in Porto Alegre in
January 2003. The worldwide coordination of these demonstrations thus may signal the emergence of a *global* public sphere,
of which European publics are wings, but whose heart may lie
in the Southern Hemisphere.

The philosophers' appeal suggests that Europe has a special
obligation at this historical moment to promote peace and
justice through international law, against a US policy that flouts
such internationalism. Europe must be the 'locomotive'
propelling the citizens of the world on their journey toward
cosmopolitan democracy. Using the international institutions
of the United Nations, economic summits such as G8 meetings, and the World Trade Organization, the International
Monetary Fund, and the World Bank, the core states of Europe
'should exert [their] influence in shaping the design for a
coming global domestic policy.'

Certainly Europe should exert its influence, especially
against efforts of the United States to bypass or sever the thin
threads of international connection that international policies
have spun in the last half-century. The image that I derive
from this injunction to use the public fora of the UN, WTO,
IMF, and economic summits, however, conjures meetings of
advanced industrial states of the Northern hemisphere in
political contestation with one another. In this image, most of
the world's people watch the North American and European

rivals debating; a few other countries temporarily enter the discussion on one side or the other. From the point of view of most of the world's people, that is, Europe's confrontation with the United States may look like sibling rivalry. If the hegemony of the United States should be confronted and resisted, and it should, why not enlist the efforts of the peoples of Africa, Asia, and Latin America, as well as Europe, from the beginning?

In order for Europe to carry out its global mission as engine of the cosmopolitan train, Habermas says that Europeans must forge a stronger sense of European identity that transcends the parochialism of national identity. Many of the institutions and values that originated in Europe, such as Christianity, capitalism, science, democracy, and human rights, he says, have proliferated beyond Europe. A European identity for today can be culled from the distinctively reflexive way that European societies have responded to the problems generated by modernity, nationalism, and capitalist expansion. In the welfare state Europeans have developed a solution to the inequalities generated by capitalism, and European states have managed to maintain standards of welfare in the face of strong globalizing economic pressures to change. Europeans also have already begun to put the aggressive dangers of nationalism behind them by instituting the European Union. These successes can and should serve as exemplars to the world.

A European identity, however, cannot exist unless there are others from whom it is differentiated. The call to embrace a particularist European identity, then, means constructing a new distinction between insiders and outsiders. Habermas's main concern is to distinguish a European identity from America. 'For us, a president who opens his daily business with public prayer, and associates his significant political decisions with a divine mission, is hard to imagine.' Other others, in the East and South, stand in the shadows, perhaps, huddled at the edges of this playground where the big boys call each other names. And what of the other within? Is a European identity expansive enough to include the millions of children of Asian and African descent whose parents and grandparents have migrated to the metropole? Like many Americans, many Europeans have reacted to recent global conflicts by distancing themselves from those they identify as foreigners. Surely invoking a European identity inhibits tolerance within and solidarity with those far away. Here I fear that Habermas may reinscribe the logic of the nation-state for Europe, rather than transcend it.

In *The Invention of the Americas*, Enrique Dussel retells the story of modernity as based on the European colonial project.[1] Having spent centuries fighting the Muslims and driving them eastward, and having discovered the treasures, power, and technical innovation of the empires in far Asia, Europe found itself on the edges of the world. The European imagination invented America, Dussel argues, as a means of putting itself back at the center. Doesn't the philosophers' appeal look like an attempt to re-center Europe? Europe will stand between the power of the United States and the interests of an inclusive global order, tempering the former and offering leadership for the latter. I agree that the hegemony of the United States should be confronted and resisted, and recent months have shown that European people and states united in that resistance have the potential to bring more balance to power. Europe cannot and should not engage in such confrontation, however, *on behalf* of the rest of the peoples of the world, but *with* them.

The appeal for a European foreign policy ends by referring to a relationship between European countries and the global South: it recalls Europe's imperial past. A hundred years ago the great European nations experienced the 'bloom' of imperial power. Since then their power has declined and Europeans have experienced the 'loss' of empire. This experience of decline, Habermas says, has allowed Europeans to become reflexive. 'They could learn from the perspective of the defeated to perceive themselves in the dubious role of victors who are called to account for the violence of a forcible and uprooting process of modernization.'

In this reflection I hear Habermas invite his audience in their imaginations to adopt the perspective of formerly colonized others, and learn to look at Europe and Europeans from that perspective. Certainly engaging in such an exercise is better than being self-absorbed, as one might assert is the United States and are many Americans. But wouldn't it be better to have real discussions with people and states of the South and East on the sort of equal basis that might tell Europeans (and Americans) things they may not wish to hear about their biases and duties? Where is the forum that Europe has entered to be held accountable?

Referring to colonialism and imperialism as an 'uprooting process of modernization' makes it sound like colonialism is an unfortunate byproduct of the otherwise universalistic and enlightened project Europe led to establish the principles of human rights, rule of law, and expanded productivity. Colonialism was not just a vicious process of modernization, but a system of slavery and labor exploitation. What are the signs that European people and states have responded to a call for accountability with gestures of contrition and reparation?

As an American, I and others like me have distinct responsibilities to resist the US government's unilateral policies and push for positive change. Citizens of European states have their own responsibilities toward their states and the policies of the European Union. Rather than reposition Europe as a central player in global politics, however, the progressive project ought to be, in the phrase of Dipesh Chakrabarty, to *provincialize* Europe (as well as the United States).[2] Peoples from all parts of the globe, and especially from those parts whose people are most excluded and dominated by American- and European-led capital processes, ought to sit on terms of equality that recognize the particularity of each to work on solutions to global problems.

The fora at which Habermas proposes that Europe might exert its influence against the current dangerous unilateralist thrust of US foreign policy all tend to privilege the global

North and dominate the global South. The structure of the United Nations Security Council privileges the five permanent members. The constitutions of the International Monetary Fund and the World Bank give more power and influence to wealthy countries than poor ones. Many peoples of the Southern hemisphere suffer the consequences of crushing debt and micro-economic coercion imposed by some of these international institutions, in the name of fiscal responsibility and the stabilization of currency markets. Shouldn't the project of cosmopolitan democracy raise the question of the reform or abolition of these institutions?

Global inequalities are not merely a legacy of colonialism, but result from ongoing structural processes that daily widen the gap between those with nothing and those living in privileged affluence. While even the poorest country has rich people, and affluent countries have poor people, most of those who can assume affluent comfort as a way of life dwell in North America and Europe. Without question European countries do better than the United States in providing meaningful transfers to redress these inequalities. Even Europe's generosity in this regard is, however, pitifully low and along with that of the United States has been declining since 1990.

The privileges of wealth, social order, consumer comfort, well-developed infrastructure, strong capacity to finance government activity, and solidaristic culture make European states and citizens well positioned to take leadership in the project of strengthening international law and peaceful conflict resolution, and instituting mechanisms of global redistribution. Certainly they should exert influence to pressure, shame, and encourage the United States and its citizens to join in this project. We are taking no steps toward cosmopolitan democracy, however, if the many other peoples of the world do not have influential seats at a table that holds the powerful accountable to the poor and affords real influence to less affluent regions. The weekend of February 15, 2003 signaled a global public sphere that existed before then and has persisted. Many

European and North American participants in global civil
society look to activists from Brazil or Kenya or India or Sri
Lanka for insight and leadership. A democratic European
foreign policy would listen across an empty center to those and
other Southern voices in a circle of equality.

Frankfurter Rundschau, July 22, 2003

---

[1] Enrique Dussel, *The Invention of the Americas: Eclipse of 'the Other' and the Invention of Modernity* (New York: Continuum, 1995).

[2] Dipesh Chakrabarty, *Provincializing Europe: Postcolonial Thought and Historical Difference* (Princeton University Press: Princeton, 2000).

WHO CAME UP WITH THE IDEA OF A 'CORE EUROPE'?

Gerd Langguth

Finally, a debate about Europe among intellectuals! *Quo vadis*, Europe? Now, even eloquent authors and scholars of the old continent concern themselves with a question that is by no means new. In fact, it has preoccupied the minds of visionaries for centuries. The idea of a 'core Europe,' now propagated again, is in fact an age-old one. When Saint-Simon and Thierry published their vision of a European *avant-garde* in 1814,[1] they could already fall back upon the reflections of Sully from the era of the Thirty Years War, and those of Saint-Pierre, but also upon those by Kant from the eighteenth century.

Searching for a New Identity

For a long time, the basis for arguments in favor of the European Union was largely technocratic and economic. And, hitherto, there have been some spokesmen who actually feared a culturally unified Europe. Now renowned intellectuals are eager to contribute to the project of making Europe meaningful to everyone. Slogans and catchphrases such as the 'Birth of a European Public,' 'Europe's Rebirth,' and 'Europe is that which Europe will become' are used. The European people, who for centuries had repeatedly confronted each other in armed conflicts, are nowadays supposed to give the signal for a 'world domestic policy.'

Do the protagonists, such as the widely recognized German philosopher Jürgen Habermas, mean all the peoples of Europe?

The answer: No, not all! The stubborn British, and some East-Central Europeans, resist a 'European Identity' as the German scholar sketches it out. For that reason, he pleads for the formation of an '*avant-garde* core Europe,' gathered around Germany and France, that is supposed to finally have an effective common foreign and security policy and that allows, in the period following, for holdout dissenting states to join eventually.

Bush as a Polarizing Element

With this demand, Habermas appropriates the apparently prominent theses of politicians about core Europe (see the article by Lamers and Schäuble, and the Humboldt University speech by Joschka Fischer[2]), namely the ideas that some nations in Europe progress faster than others, but that those faster ones will keep the door open for all those wishing to enter the Core-House. The discussion about a 'two-speed' Europe has enriched the European debate for years and is, in both theory and practice, by no means new in individual political arenas. Unlike previous discussions about core Europe, the debate that Habermas initiated has an anti-American sentiment to it. As an independent power, Europe is supposed to create a unique image for itself not in accordance with, but in distinction from the United States. Such a discourse, as Habermas desires it, in the current situation led rather to a fission of Europeans.

It is truly a good feeling when even philosophers now speculate about the spiritual foundations of European integration. But what is striking about Habermas is that the predominant element in his theses about Europe is an anti-Americanism, disguised as 'anti-Bushism.' Yet can a European identity establish itself primarily *ex negativo*? Even the supposedly common characteristics of European nations which Habermas represented affirmatively (such as, for example, individualism, rationalism, the ideological neutrality of state authority, the greater trust in the controlling capacities of the state, scepticism about the competitiveness of the market) appear in his manifesto more like the reflexes of an 'old European' affronted by Donald Rumsfeld's words, rather than as a sober inventory.

Habermas's article is a text profoundly influenced by the German experience. The characteristics it mentions, at any rate, are in themselves hardly enough to allow the European population to suddenly discover 'an attractive, even inspiring vision of a future Europe.' Habermas himself has to admit that many European achievements, precisely as a result of their world-wide success, have lost some of their power to create an identity for Europe. And in the US, the 'New World,' the democratic consequences of the French Revolution had already become a constitutional reality at a time when dictatorships or autocracies still ruled in most European countries.

How much the anti-American perspective is constitutive for Habermas's notion of a European identity is evident in his elevation of the demonstrations against the Iraq war on February 15, 2003 to the status of a potential 'birth of a European public.' The support for overcoming violence in international relations – which Habermas, by referring to these demonstrations, apparently wishes to confirm as a genuinely European gesture – is, however, a global phenomenon, and supported by people all around the world. People didn't take to the streets only in London, Rome, Madrid, Berlin, and Paris but also in Calcutta, Melbourne, São Paulo, and also, lest we forget, in New York. Habermas's theses sound very much like an attempt to initiate the birth of a European nationalism fueled by a basic resentment of America.

A Diversity Difficult to Overcome

I do not doubt Habermas's sympathies for a supposedly European social model. However, he does not mention that the 'model' he favors obviously does not at present have any convincing instruments for management at its disposal in, for example, the battle against unemployment. Indisputably, there are different political and cultural traditions in the US and in Europe respectively, yet these are also highly divergent within

Europe itself. Just think of the various forms of state interven-
tionism in France, where to this very day the state has a
tremendous influence on economic activity. In Germany, on
the other hand, the state keeps more and more out of the
economy despite its authoritarian tradition, not to mention the
example of Great Britain.

The unified European economic model that Habermas
would like us to believe in is therefore a chimera. Herbert
Marcuse, another representative of the 'Frankfurt School,' once
said that 'inherent in negation itself is already the positive.' A
European identity based primarily on the negation of the
American political model will never be feasible. Furthermore,
Habermas, to a great extent, does not take into account the
practical elements of European everyday life that are tangible
and support the creation of identity: borders and border controls
have disappeared almost completely; goods can be imported
and exported between EU countries without any obstacles; the
European job market is remarkable for its high mobility; there
are extensive high school and university exchange programs;
and the citizens have standardized passports and driver's licenses.
Most EU countries have recently adopted a common currency
– a not insignificant means of identification if one keeps in
mind how much the strong German mark shaped the national
pride of West Germans in postwar Germany.

Neue Zürcher Zeitung, August 12, 2003

---

[1] The utopian socialist thinker and the historian collaborated on a work
  entitled 'De la réorganisation de la société européenne,' published in
  1814. It envisioned a politically and institutionally homogeneous
  European state.

[2] German prime minister Joschka Fischer's well-known address at
  Humboldt University on May 12, 2000, appears in English translation
  as 'From Confederacy to Federation: Thoughts on the Finality of
  European Integration' at the official website of the German foreign
  ministry: www.auswaertiges-amt.de.

3

FURTHER REFLECTIONS

THE IRAQ WAR:
Critical Reflections from 'Old Europe'

Ulrich K. Preuss

On August 24, 1814, English troops occupied Washington, the capital of the newly founded and still fragile United States of America. The troops, led by General Robert Ross and Admiral Sir George Cockburn, deliberately burned down all public buildings, including the Capitol and the White House. General Ross personally supervised the soldiers who piled up the furniture from the White House and then set it on fire. The well-disciplined troops were ordered to leave private property untouched. Among the public buildings, only the patent office was spared. The wily director of the office had convinced Ross that the patents stored there were the private property of their inventors. President Madison and his administration were forced to flee to neighboring Virginia. Madison never recovered from this humiliation. More importantly, the event remained engraved into the nation's collective memory. Washington in flames became the tangible and material evidence that even the blessings of the geographical distance from Europe, with its multiple quarrels and wars, could not fully protect the American Republic. Staying away from Europe was a fundamental political principle of the young republic. 'Why,' George Washington asked in his Farewell Address on September 17, 1796, 'by interweaving our destiny with that of any part of Europe, entangle our peace and prosperity in the toils of European ambition, rivalry, interest, humor or caprice?' He promptly answered his rhetorical question: 'It is our true policy to steer clear of

permanent alliances with any portion of the foreign world.'
Being a realist, he added that this posture only applies insofar
'as we are now at liberty to do it.'

This doctrine marks the core of a powerful and sometimes
dominant current of American foreign policy. In a study of
the history of American foreign policy published toward the
end of the last century, James Chace and Caleb Carr characterized this foreign-policy tenor as 'the quest for absolute
security.'[1] Absolute security means independence from any
power or alliance, friendly or not, in matters of national
security. The exemplary counterconcept was the widely criticized European model of relative security. This balance-of-
power model had emerged from the logic of the Westphalian
order. The external security of states was made dependent on
the mutual balancing of power, on shifting alliances and skillful
maneuvering, diplomatic finesse, cunning intrigues, treacheries,
and cold-blooded interest calculations by different actors in a
game full of plotting and scheming. However repugnant and
cynical this system may seem to us, it contained an early form
of a system of collective security insofar as national security is
thought to be possible only in relation to and in cooperation
with other states. Given this history, it should not surprise us
that the American proponents of the concept of absolute security have seen – and probably continue to see – the contrast
with the European model not only as a political and strategic
difference, but also in terms of a moral contrast. America was
the embodiment of the universal republic, founded on reason,
self-evident truths, and inalienable rights. In contrast, the
Europe of the dynasties, with their courtly etiquette, intrigues,
and diplomatic hair-splitting, represented the dark and backward past from which the Pilgrim Fathers and many other
upright, honest men and women had fled. The geographical
distance between the US and Europe corresponded to a superiority vis-à-vis the old continent. This sense of superiority was
ultimately based upon the deep religious conviction of being
a newly chosen people. At first glance, it is startling that in

spite of this geographically and historically grounded philosophy of foreign-policy self-sufficiency, the US was drawn into
foreign conflicts in Europe and other distant corners of the
earth. To be sure, we need to take into account not only the
general doctrine, but also Washington's caveat that there will
always be geopolitical situations in which the US cannot afford
to abstain from close political alliances with other nations. The
time of the Cold War – between the Second World War and
the fall of the Berlin Wall – was certainly a period in which
pure isolation was not tenable. Still, a closer examination reveals
that US global intervention did not occur in spite of this
doctrine, but because of it. Absolute security demands nothing
less than the control of all forces that could potentially endanger
the territorial integrity or political independence of the nation.
In an increasingly interdependent world, such dangers might
be posed by states far from the US. The insistence on complete
independence forecloses the option of making national security dependent on relationships of trust or even friendship with
other states. The quest for absolute security therefore tends,
according to Chace and Carr, to support military reactions to
perceived threats. For this reason, Americans have never shied
away from using unilateral force as a means of protecting
national security in regions they perceived as a vital threat. The
intervention in Afghanistan is only the most recent instance of
a refusal to put national security interests into the hands of an
alliance. This unilateralism is the flipside of the genuinely
American principle of relying on one's own strength to solve
problems. But the imperative of absolute security has the disquieting attribute of being internally unbounded. Whoever strives
for invulnerability based on his own power must extend the
realm of his control indefinitely and yet will never feel
completely safe. Absolute security will only arrive when
nothing changes anymore and we are at the End of History.
This might be the reason why Francis Fukuyama's *End of History*
became so popular in the United States.[2] The promise of the
book's title might as well have been 'Absolute Security.'

It is not a coincidence that Fukuyama's thesis of the end of history was premised on the final victory of liberal democracy over all competing systems of government. In fact, the world might be made significantly safer if elementary forms of self-determination, the rule of law, and human rights protections existed in all states. But the world is not that perfect. Whoever demands perfect security in an imperfect world invariably faces enigmas. Most importantly, whoever demands perfect security in an imperfect world is a problem for others. A nation claiming the privilege of absolute security for itself will tend to see some despotic regimes as threats to its national security and will insist on its right to rid the world of them by military means. The United States can do this in a much more unabashed manner since – unlike Europe – it does not see a contradiction between state sovereignty and human rights. Did not the founding fathers declare the right to political self-determination a fundamental human right? How can liberating a people, if necessary by military means, be construed as a violation of sovereignty? Accordingly, the national-security rationale for the intervention is reinforced by a universalistic legal and moral principle.

Robert Kagan has rightly claimed that Americans and Europeans have different perspectives on international politics. The phrase 'old Europe,' brought up by the US Secretary of Defense, is only the polemical dramatization of a quintessentially correct analysis. Contemporary Europe's visions of international security are in fact a continuation of the old dynastic system of balancing power among equally sovereign states – adapted to the democratic age, to be sure, but the principle is still the same. The international law framework of the United Nations is the appropriate current form of this old principle. It is a system of collective security that incorporates potential aggressors into a network of common obligations, institutions, and procedures, thereby creating trust and transforming the international state of nature into an international legal condition. The philosophical origins of this concept lie in Immanuel Kant's 'federation of free republics,' but, paradoxically, the political institutionalization of this concept was initiated by Woodrow Wilson, an American president. In the US, Wilson does not enjoy a particularly good reputation. His idea of the League of Nations was never quite popular in the US. It is one of the great ironies in history that the president who created the League of Nations could not convince his nation to become a member. Yet this is not a break with US foreign-policy traditions. The reason why the US never joined the League of Nations is that the Senate refused to ratify the Treaty of Versailles – the first 26 Articles of this treaty were simultaneously the statute of the League of Nations. George Washington posthumously won against Woodrow Wilson.

The differences between American and European views about the order of world politics are thus deeply rooted in the history of international relations. It should not come as a surprise that these differences resurfaced during the Iraq crisis. In this situation, the two concepts of security clashed directly: the concept of relative security with the UN model of collective security on the one hand, and the concept of absolute security based on the unilateral protection of national security on the other hand. During the intervention in Afghanistan that followed September 11, 2001, these two approaches could still be brought into convergence. The Europeans gained the reassurance of two UN Security Council resolutions that authorized the military actions as an exercise of the right to self-defense pursuant to Article 51 of the UN Charter. The Americans, in contrast, assumed the existence of a situation triggering the duties of assistance among NATO partners according to Article 5 of the NATO Treaty. Once their troops were on the ground, however, they politely but firmly refused any assistance offered by NATO partners, with the justification that their own military capacities permitted them to go it alone. Both sides had good reasons for claiming that they were remaining true to their respective principles while in perfect agreement with the other side. The dissonances between the US and 'old' Europe that were already apparent during the

Afghanistan crisis have deepened tremendously during the Iraq crisis. The issue was not, as it seemed to the casual observer, the choice between war and peace. The actual stakes of this transatlantic dispute can only be seen once we acknowledge the real point of disagreement: war according to the criteria of the US, or war according to the legality of the UN? How is this choice to be understood?

Military measures can only be in accordance with the UN Charter if they are 'military sanctions' authorized by the UN Security Council in cases where nonmilitary means of conflict resolution have failed – setting aside for the moment the right to self-defense under Article 51, which cannot justify an intervention in Iraq. These military sanctions are coercive measures that the international legal community can take against member-states that breach or threaten international peace or security. Since the UN does not have its own troops, member-states acting on the basis of a Security Council authorization execute these coercive measures. The external appearance of these 'measures' exhibits all the characteristics of war: the blind destructive force of military might certainly does not fail to register in such cases. Yet there is a good reason why the UN Charter avoids the terminology of war in this context. The 'military measures' are, strictly speaking, no longer wars in the classical sense. The classical notion of war is that of an exercise of force between states that, due to the lack of a common law and a common judge, settle their disputes over legal claims or legally protected interests through the exercise of military might.

According to these criteria, military measures on the basis of Security Council resolutions are not wars because the UN Charter is a legal order binding on all nations and thus capable of providing legally ordered procedures for conflict resolution. The most extreme of these legal measures for resolving disputes are the 'military sanctions' mentioned above; they represent an embryonic form of police measures taken by a community against those members derelict in their duties. This type of force is aimed at the re-establishment of a damaged legal order. This conception might explain why many people do not view 'military measures' authorized by the Security Council as moral catastrophes on a par with 'real wars.' At least, as we saw again in the case of Iraq, these military sanctions trigger significantly less resistance than pure wars among states. If the suffering of the victims were the yardstick, such a differentiation would not be very convincing. Even though measures authorized by the Security Council fulfill a police function, their use of force is essentially a military one. The purpose of the use of force in police operations is strictly limited to warding off dangers, with the permissible means restricted accordingly. The aim of police operations is to incapacitate individual authors of threats to public safety. Military operations, in contrast, are aimed against an entire country and its inhabitants. Even if international law declares only military objects legitimate targets, this restriction is not very effective, given the current complex interconnections between civilian and military infrastructure. The so-called collateral damage to civilians and civilian infrastructure can easily exceed the damage to military targets, as we saw in the war in Kosovo. In the case of Iraq, the mix between police functions and military attributes that characterizes the UN-sanctioned 'military measures' leads to complicated self-contradictions.

Iraq was ruled by a hideous regime headed by a brutal autocrat. It was pressured to destroy weapons of mass destruction that experts had good reason to believe existed within its boundaries. Severe measures, including military sanctions, were used as threats in the case of non-compliance. However, there is no definitive knowledge as to whether the regime possessed such weapons, or how many. Even if it had been known with certainty that the regime possessed such weapons, military measures would not have been advisable. In that case, military measures would only have provoked the use of the weapons of mass destruction by a regime that was virtually unsurpassed in unscrupulousness. At the very least, a ground invasion would

have been ruled out. This was the rationale for the – not implaus-
ible – argument of those who asserted that the US was preparing
for war against Iraq, despite the fact that the existence of weapons
of mass destruction there remained uncertain, while at the same
time it negotiated with North Korea, another regime belonging
to the 'axis of evil,' but one which was certainly in possession
of such weapons. On the other hand, military measures against
Iraq could also have been ruled out if one had known with
certainty that the regime did not possess such weapons. In this
case, it would have been likely that the regime could not have
used weapons of mass destruction or passed them on to terrorist
groups. In order to eliminate this uncertainty, UN inspectors
worked to scrutinize the country's facilities. Had the inspectors
never found such weapons, there would have been no *casus belli*.
Had they ever located such weapons, there would have been
strong reasons against the war as well, since this danger could
have been most effectively removed by forcing the country to
destroy them – or taking their own steps to destroy them.
Military enforcement of disarmament would only be warranted
if the country violently resisted the destruction of weapons
found. But this case never arose.

The only remaining possible justification for military action
within the UN framework could be the use of military measures in order to force the Iraqi regime to disclose its weapons
arsenals so that the world might finally have full certainty about
Iraq's weapons of mass destruction. In fact, domestic regulations of police conduct usually provide for the authorized use
of force at the suspicion of a grave danger. For example, if
there is uncertainty about whether all animals in a given herd
of cattle are infected with mad-cow disease, the police may kill
all the animals in order to protect the life and health of
consumers. But is it possible to lead a war without the certainty
that there is a *casus belli*? Is a 'war grounded on a reasonable
suspicion' imaginable?

In this situation fraught with uncertainties, the conduct of
some governments poses further questions. Even after the EU

members agreed on a common position on February 17, 2003, the German government – more precisely, the Chancellor and, in a more roundabout way, the foreign minister – strictly rejected the use of force in Iraq, irrespective of the results of the UN weapons inspections. At the same time, the Chancellor and the foreign minister supported the US threat of military force as a means of buttressing the work of the inspectors. So far, however, neither of them has explained the feasibility of a strategy that pressures a regime to cooperate by military threats while simultaneously issuing assurances that the threat of force will under no circumstances – not even in the case of persistent non-cooperation – be transformed into an actual use of force. On the other hand, there is the question why the US fiercely insisted on proving the existence of weapons of mass destruction in Iraq and tried to force Saddam Hussein to admit the existence of such weapons, while at the same time it became apparent that war against Iraq would be waged irrespective of the results of the UN inspections. Given these circumstances, what incentives for cooperating with the US could the dictator possibly have had in a situation in which he seemed unable to prevent his own downfall?

Quite obviously, a war aimed at the disarmament of a state merely suspected of having weapons – it is even less certain whether the weapons, which were last sighted five years ago, are still functional – cannot be justified. War is despicable even for people who are not committed pacifists. War is, as the preamble to the UN Charter expresses rightly and with pathos, 'a scourge, which … has brought untold sorrow to mankind.' War is a rupture of civilization; war embodies the negation of basic principles of well-ordered societies. The logic of war implies the indiscriminate killing of persons, and the destruction of the natural environment, infrastructure, food-stuff, and cultural artifacts. War implements the principle of collective responsibility that the modern world in its legal–moral development has long overcome. The legal recognition of war is restricted to its elementary form: the natural right to self-defense against an armed aggression. Under no circumstances may war be conducted as 'the continuation of politics by other means,' as Clausewitz could naively define it in the early nineteenth century.

Even those motivated by justified anger or benign calculations who seek to employ military force for the destruction of an abhorrent regime will inevitably be entangled in the moral contradiction that war – in its indiscriminate character effectively indistinguishable from collective punishment – will invariably kill and injure innocents. Given the empirical evidence, war will in all likelihood harm more innocent people than guilty ones. Which moral reasons could justify the death of so many innocent persons as the price for the punishment and dethronement of a few culprits?

To pose the reverse question: was it morally justified to exclude the sanction of war against Iraq under all circumstances, irrespective of the results of the neutral inspectors' examinations of the destructive capabilities of the regime? After all, there might have been a chance that the Iraqi regime, which could be counted on to be unscrupulous, would have tried to hold the entire Gulf region, including Israel, hostage in order to force its will on the world. In such a situation, how much should America risk, and how much should Europe risk? Is North Korea not enough of a warning? In the case of this sinister regime, which is driving its own population to the verge of starvation, and in contrast to Iraq, we need not rely on speculation. Obviously, even a regime of UN inspections could not prevent North Korea from gaining possession of nuclear weapons, and from threatening South Korea, Japan, and even the United States. Even though neither Iraq nor North Korea possesses systems capable of delivering nuclear warheads beyond their respective regions, how can we be certain that networks of suicide bombers that exist in different parts of the globe could not be converted into human carriers or mobile launching sites for nuclear bombs? After September 11, is this still merely science fiction?

A war started without due consideration of the good reasons cautioning against it is morally unjustified. But a peace without due consideration of the good reasons cautioning against it is also morally unjustified.

The only issue we could and should have argued about is: which risks was the world willing to take in the face of an Iraqi regime threatening to use weapons of mass destruction and thereby forcing its will on the international legal community? We need to demand the calm sobriety of a world police capable of weighing risks and dangers. The greater the potential damage from weapons of mass destruction in the hands of the Iraqi regime, the smaller we needed to keep the likelihood of the occurrence of this scenario. As such calculations remind us, war harbors risks, but so does peace. The risks of a war are: the destruction of a country, its infrastructure, and its oil wells; harm to hundreds of thousands of civilians; and in addition the possibility of a political explosion in a region already wrought with crises, where Israel still faces neighbors threatening its extinction. The risks of the peace are: attacks still more devastating than the ones of September 11; the persistent threat posed by further attacks possibly more intense in their malicious destructive force; the permanent threat of the death of thousands of people due to the now easily available 'small' weapons of mass destruction; and the increasing vulnerability to blackmail by criminal regimes and their terrorist support squads.

Accordingly, the justification of a war of disarmament against Iraq did not require a 'smoking gun,' the piece of evidence in criminal law that would prove the existence of functional weapons of mass destruction in the hands of the Iraqi regime 'beyond reasonable doubt.' On the other hand, a merely abstract danger that the regime could possess such weapons, use them, or pass them on to terrorist groups was not a sufficient justification for an act as grave and far-reaching as war. Since we need to rely on complex calculations of risk and the balancing of interests, we need to examine the stakes more carefully. What are the implications of the simple fact that the price for liberating a people from brutal dictatorship is the death of many innocent civilians? If a people liberates itself from illegitimate rule through a rebellion or revolution, it is proper to say that the people are taking their fate in their own hands; they take responsibility for the sacrifices necessary for achieving their goal. This case is different from the scenario in which these liberties are introduced from abroad through a military intervention by more or less altruistic third parties. John Stuart Mill, like many nineteenth-century liberals, argued that a people needs to fight for its own freedom. Freedom cannot be imposed or granted from abroad.[3] Given the experiences of totalitarian conditions, this position might seem too demanding or even frivolous, since such regimes have superior means of force over the human body and soul. The implication would be that a people living under such circumstances might need to wait for many generations until it is liberated.

Moreover, a people living under totalitarian rule cannot express its opinion on whether it would like to be liberated or not, and what price it would be willing to pay. Without doing violence to the facts on the ground, one can assume that no people, including the Iraqi people bent and brutalized during forty years of one-party rule, will voluntarily renounce basic human rights guarantees – however problematic the use of the term 'voluntary' might be. On the other hand, among the masses of the people the desire for liberation is never so strong and absolute that any price for liberty would be acceptable. Thus, the brightly shining moral reasons for the change of the criminal regime are dimmed by considerations about the price of the liberation. These considerations are all the more important since it is not the liberated but the liberator that unilaterally dictates the price that is overwhelmingly to be paid by the to-be-liberated. This dilemma demonstrates the full range of moral ambiguities surrounding the issue of liberating a people from the rule of a wicked and illegitimate regime through military force. Given these considerations, it is not surprising that the

permissibility of humanitarian interventions is hotly contested
among international lawyers and practitioners of international
politics. Even those who generally recognize the protection of
basic human rights and minimum standards of civilizational
achievements as grounds for a legal military intervention are
careful to formulate a number of restrictive conditions. Among
these conditions is that military intervention be strictly necessary: military interventions are only permissible as a last resort
after all other available means for ending mass human rights
violations are exhausted.[4] The cause of human rights, though
a morally unambiguous good, needs to demonstrate its feasibility in real life. Paradoxically, the cause of human rights fares
best in these tests when the implementation of human rights
seems the lesser evil in the real-world circumstances. It is only
this realism that prevents the highflying or even arrogant
idealism of human rights from losing touch with real existing
people and their needs.

Another part of the feasibility test that human rights claims
for intervention have to face is the consideration of the consequences of humanitarian intervention on the international
political order. Such intervention is an encroachment on state
sovereignty as protected by international law, so there is additional warrant for a cautious approach. The sovereignty of states
should not be seen as an absolute, even if only because it is
too often a shield that ruthless dictators like Saddam Hussein
use to protect themselves from international scrutiny and secure
impunity for malicious crimes. On the other hand, the equal
sovereignty of all states, be they small, poor, and powerless or
big, wealthy, and powerful, is an important step in the direction of civilizing international affairs. In the absence of an
international community of equal and sovereign states, the
world would fall back into the state of nature where the natural
right of the strongest is supreme. In the democratic age, the
respect for state sovereignty also entails the respect for the right
to self-determination of the people organized in the state. Still,
according to standing international law, non-democratic states

also have a claim to the recognition of their sovereignty. In these cases, international law faces a tension between the promotion of human rights and the recognition of equal state sovereignty. Our moral intuitions would lead us to solve this tension in favor of human rights. However, in the world of states there is no court standing above all states that could lend validity to the moral and legal principles recognized by all. In order to secure a minimum of order and predictability in international affairs, we must accordingly continue to affirm the morally neutral principle of state sovereignty as the basic ordering principle of international politics. State sovereignty equally protects democratic and non-democratic states from interventions and is thus unsatisfactory from a moral point of view. Were this principle to hold sway completely, the world would be forced to stand aside passively while rulers deny the people their liberty and their modest share in the achievements of human civilization.

In order to avoid these consequences, the international legal community increasingly favors a cautious restriction of state sovereignty in order to protect fundamental human rights. Still, the same additional restrictions apply here that we discussed in the context of liberating humanitarian interventions: the sacrifices that are typically to be made by the liberated need to be taken into account, and we need to apply the standard of strict necessity. Only when there is a reasonable chance that the long-term benefits of an encroachment on state sovereignty will be higher than the damage to the international order, and if it can be assumed that the intervention will improve the human rights situation in the long run, is a humanitarian intervention justified.

Taking these considerations as a yardstick, it is very questionable whether the US intervention in Iraq met the requirements for a justified intervention. Here we must disregard the knowledge we gained from the war and after the war: it is the situation of uncertainty before the war that is decisive. We have many indications that economic and political pressure

on the regime aiming at improving fundamental human rights
was by no means exhausted. One could even say that options
in this direction were barely explored, since all non-military
pressures on the regime were aimed at controlling the stock-
piling of weapons of mass destruction. As a consequence, the
situation was not one in which the military intervention was
the *ultima ratio* for the protection of human rights.

Irrespective of such considerations about balancing uncertainty and risk, the Americans were determined to go to war,
while the Germans were determined to oppose it. We may
thus assume that these inconsistencies reveal motivations that
follow a different logic than that of the function of a world
police warding off dangers to the international community.
Since the German position will not influence the course of
history, let us focus on the determination of the Americans to
go to war against Iraq. Why didn't the Americans want to
realize that the world would be in a more civilized state if the
US had committed its superior military capacities to the service
of the UN and, like a world police, took military measures
only in accordance with the Security Council's assessment of
the risks and dangers?

The answer to this question is as simple as it is painful to
the Europeans: the US military is being used unilaterally
because the US military and the resources that US society desig-
nated for its use are primarily, if not solely, dedicated to the
goal of protecting national security; and because the Americans,
as we have seen, traditionally do not make their national
security dependent on the decisions of other states, and will
certainly not put it in the hands of international institutions.
The hyperpower of the United States, lacking a serious geopolitical rival, does not act as the trustee of the international
community, nor is it motivated by the vision of restoring the
integrity of the international legal order jeopardized by the
lawless Iraqi regime. Rather, the US perceives the establishment of a new world order to be the primary challenge.
According to this view, the events of September 11 clearly and

brutally demonstrated the necessity of a new world order. This day became an 'international constitutional moment' for the world, but especially for America, as an American lawyer recently stated: a rapid, sudden, extraordinary, and dramatic overthrow of the old order. On the rubble of this old order, something new must be built. We are only starting to understand the character of this new order.

Without much sentimentality, the US faces the fact that now, for the first time since the humiliation of August 24, 1814, when Washington stood in flames, it cannot provide reliable security to its people within its territory. This recognition comes in a historical period that marks the peak of US military might, unrivaled by any other power. (To give just one example: the air force second in size to the US Air Force is that of the US Navy.) More systematically and consistently than ever before, the US government is pursuing the goal of achieving security at home through the exercise of power in many faraway regions around the globe, while these efforts are simultaneously met with deep hatred in many parts of the world. America sees itself as forced into the role of an order-creating world power that is ultimately responsible for international security in a global civilization crippled by fragmentation, state disintegration, and global terrorism. It is not a coincidence that more thoughtful American discourse increasingly discusses whether the US is becoming an empire – a globally dominant power in possession of a rule spanning nations, bearing all the corresponding burdens and responsibilities. If one follows this perspective for a moment, one needs to add that at least the US is becoming an empire against its will, driven instead by the internal logic of an expansive and insatiable drive for absolute security, incapable of investing trust in others. Louis Begley writes that he is especially proud of one quality of the American empire, which is that it, in contradistinction to the disintegrated Soviet empire, rests on states that want to be allies and parts of the empire.[5] While Begley's distinction between the American and Soviet empires seems unobjectionable, it poses the question whether an 'empire of allies' is not an impossible constellation. Allies are in relationships of equal rights and equal footing, mutual respect, voluntary cooperation, and, most of all, mutual trust. How can such a concept be reconciled with the unilateral and hierarchical power of an empire over satellite states?

Once we view the United States as an empire, we can plausibly solve the puzzle of why the Americans were seemingly determined to go to war regardless of the results of inspections. Thus, it is not the cowboy mentality that Europeans like to ascribe to Americans, nor an unresolved father–son relationship in the Bush family, nor the interest in oil – the favorite topic of all geopolitical strategists posing as realists – that would explain the persistent US insistence to go to war, but rather the US resolution to establish a new world order. This world order will not be the international legal community of the United Nations armed with police-like authorities. Rather, this is the order of a strange and unique empire. This empire connects the universal ideas of human rights and democracy to the very particular religious notion of the chosen American people and its historic mission of bringing democracy to the world. It might have been precisely this feeling of being the chosen ones that gave the generation of the American founders the best reasons for protecting national security like a sanctuary even from the co-determination of democratic allies.

Accordingly, the American empire is an almost inescapable consequence of American unilateralism, and of the diffuse feeling of the historic mission of the American people. For the last half-century, we Europeans have lived quite comfortably in the enjoyment of liberties that were fought for and guaranteed by America. For us, the empire was a friendly one. Empires, however, have their unique political logic. They are not, as Begley assumes, alliances among equals. According to the laws of empire, it is entirely legitimate to force regime change in a country falling within the empire's sphere of interest and influence. In the UN Charter, such action is categorically ruled out. The logic of empire accordingly implies that the UN requirements of legality do not hold a special place in the considerations of the United States. Michael Ignatieff, who is certainly no proponent of the current Bush administration's policies, expresses a widespread mood when he writes that America feels like Gulliver: an imperial giant whom European dwarfs in their legalistic fervor try to bind with the thin threads of law in order to prevent it from achieving its mission.[5]

This view has its own logic, which is the logic of Thomas Hobbes: in order for law to exist, there needs to be an order that provides law with social validity. America's war against Iraq would then be a war for the creation of a new world order whose law is not yet visible. This logic also implies that the new order, like any order based exclusively on power, tends not to be constrained by law. Law creates trust, predictability, security; law enables. The power that rejects law as a source for its validity in order to rely on violence alone will rob itself of an extension of its potential opportunities through reciprocity. Hannah Arendt, who first distinguished between communicative power and violence, could, in an analysis sharpened by an intimate knowledge of European catastrophes, teach her compatriots that the unilateral power of the lonely ruler will in the end consist of nothing more than the non-communicative violence of the military. Accordingly, American vulnerability within its state borders at the peak of its international power might not be as paradoxical as Americans tend to think. Their mute power might in fact prevent them from understanding the world around them. Power is not only a blessing. When power turns into hyperpower, it can become dangerous even to its wielder. The American political scientist Karl Deutsch coined the now famous statement that power is 'the ability to afford not to learn.' Power can be such a dangerous gift in our world! Prudent power-holders thus constrain their power and accordingly force themselves to react to the onslaught of new challenges with intelligence, creativity, perseverance, and other 'civil' attributes. Any order that does not force itself to learn gambles with its future. This is the lesson that both the Americans and the Europeans learned at the end of the eighteenth century, when they took the step from the principle of the ever-present controlling power of a hegemonic-absolutist ruler to the democratic constitutional state. It is only this change that enabled intellectual and political dispute as well as peaceful social conflict – the basis of the Euro-Atlantic model of civilization. It hardly renounces the use of power and coercion, but it tames them and makes them instruments of law.

When we think of empires, we cannot help but recall the cause of the decline of virtually all empires in world history: the overextension of their rule. Rousseau put it in words that are still valid today: 'The strongest is never strong enough to be master all the time, unless he transforms force into right and obedience into duty.'[6] There are many indications that Rousseau will continue to prevail against Hobbes. The 'old' Europe that has become wise should not become tired of showing this insight to its American friends.

Constellations 10: 3 (2003)
Translated by Christiane Wilke

[1] James Chace and Caleb Carr, *America Invulnerable: The Quest for Absolute Security from 1812 to Star Wars* (New York: Summit, 1988).
[2] Francis Fukuyama, *The End of History and the Last Man* (Harmondsworth: Penguin, 1992).
[3] John Stuart Mill, 'A Few Words on Non-Intervention,' in Mill, ed., *Dissertations and Discussions*, Vol. III (New York: Haskell House, 1873), pp. 238ff.
[4] See Peter Malanczuk, *Akehurst's Modern Introduction to International Law*, 7th ed. (London: Routledge, 1997), pp. 27f.
[5] Michael Ignatieff, 'The Virtual Commander,' *New Yorker*, August 2, 1999.
[6] Rousseau, *The Social Contract*, tr. Maurice Cranston (New York: Penguin, 1968), bk. 1, ch. 3.

POWER AND WEAKNESS IN A WORLD RISK SOCIETY

Ulrich Beck

I

It took no more than fifteen suicide bombers equipped with carpet knives to lead the world hegemonic power to a self-conception as a victim. It is, however, important to distinguish clearly between terror and terrorism, catastrophe and danger, local assassinations and a global imagination of dangers. Worldwide, various branches of industry collapse (airlines, tourism, stock prices, and insurance companies). Countries and governments are suspected of supporting terrorism and, there-fore, become the target of potential military interventions ('Axis of Evil'). The Law of Nations becomes obsolete. Alliances break, and new ones must be forged. Societies that have been civil since time immemorial turn into cultures of fear in which the borderline between justified fear and para-noia can no longer be clearly drawn. Basic democratic rights are sacrificed for the prevention of danger. *Summa summarum*: it is not physical destruction, but rather the political explosive-ness of terrorism that mass media has raised to the level of a global threat which smashes social structures. Terrorism does not win because of its horrible assassinations; rather, it wins when what is assumed to be a threat of terrorism brings the civilized world, which is built upon trust, to a collapse. That, in any case, is the perspective that the sociological theory of a world risk society affords us.

Accordingly, terrorism has already eroded the foundations of international politics. The alliances of the future, it is said, grow from the urgent questions of tomorrow and not from yesterday's blocs and institutions. Has NATO outlived itself? Will the alliance have to assume the role of world policeman in order to renew itself? National and global security policy are simultaneously demarcated and merged at the same time; the threat of terrorism rewrites the geography of power world-wide. In systematic terms, this means that the transition from a (known) international security policy to an (unknown) post-international risk policy is taking place.

This change in paradigms follows the distinction between First and Second Modernity. The classical, high-modernity of the nation-state set off a logic of policy and order that is becoming clearly recognizable only now as it is about to end, that is, since the end of the Cold War. It drew selective border-lines not only between nations and states, but also quite generally among people, things, and functional and practical realms, and created in this manner (at least, according to expectation) unambiguous institutional assignments of juris-diction, competence, and responsibility. Today, however, the following is valid: side effects of a radicalized modernization that are reflected in the public world at large create an aware-ness of new international threats. As a result of globalization and the known unpredictability of these threats to civilization, principal distinctions and basic institutions of the First Modernity disappear. What were once identifiable threats (imperial, geo-strategic, ideological, military and economic interests of powerful national states) are now replaced by the new logic of unlimited risks and insecurities that are difficult to identify (transnational terrorism, climatic catastrophe, the battle for water resources, migration currents, AIDS, the risks of genetically altered food, BSE, computer viruses that can paralyze civil and military networks of communication, etc.). Back then, we had known knowledge and corresponding predictability; now, we have (known) non-knowledge (or rather unknown non-knowledge) and corresponding unpredictability. The former requires state sovereignty; the latter repeals sovereignty. Back then, prevention followed the logic of deterrence; now, it follows the logic of interstate and post-state cooperation. This, however, means that the global conflict about the forms and contents of an 'institutionalized cosmopolitanism,' in the sense of permanent cooperation, between governmental and non-governmental protagonists begins in global and local areas such as civil social groups and nets, big companies, international organizations, the UN, churches, etc. It is certainly by no means the case that all borders and dualisms become blurred and intermingled. It is much rather precisely the other way around, namely that *demarcation forces decision*. The more demarcation, the more coercion there is to decide, and the more construction of provisional borders, permanent border policies, and border disputes. All participants – governments as well as international organizations, political parties, and civil social movements – will have to situate themselves anew in this transnational force-field in order to distribute burdens and costs, to define goals, to find ways to forge coalitions and to imagine futures of a common world, all of which results in drastic rejections and conflicts. Above all, however, a new understanding of power, dominion, and violence within the global sphere will crystallize out of generalized demarcation and insecurity. *This* is what a post-international risk policy refers to.

II

What differentiates the US and Europe are striking oppositions in their perception of danger. The terrible pictures of September 11, 2001 have etched the global threat of terrorism into the American view of the world. The wars in Afghanistan and Iraq are the first wars against a global risk. The new threat to mankind posed by nuclear terrorism completely altered the state of security before and after September 11, at least in the eyes of Americans, whereas Europeans view this new threat to mankind rather as an American hysteria. According to the opinion of the US, in the world before September 11 it would have been sufficient to do what France, Germany, Russia, China, and others had demanded: to disarm Saddam Hussein step by step. In the world after September 11, on the other hand, this is reckless and irresponsible, because even a one-percent probability that 'evil' dictators like Saddam Hussein (or disintegrating nations) pass on chemical, biological or nuclear weapons to suicide bombers is unacceptable and necessitates military action. Such a perspective entails the immanence of a denationalized, indeed, almost a socially atomized nuclear era in which what is at stake is the existence of humanity threatened by suicide bombers who will stop at nothing. For Americans, it is the horror of terrorism that reveals itself, while for Europeans it is the horror of war. Indeed, it is not comprehensible how one could try to drive out the horror of terrorism through the horror of war without evoking the apocalyptic vision of Eternal War.

Despite transatlantic differences, one parallel is, however, indeed remarkable: Just as opponents of nuclear power already consider the one-percent danger of a nuclear fallout absolutely irresponsible and, therefore, as a matter of principle, reject the peaceful use of atomic energy, many Americans already consider the one-percent probability of a terrorist use of weapons of mass destruction absolutely irresponsible and, therefore, invade Iraq (with a clear conscience).

Like those opponents of nuclear power who refer to a 'higher state of emergency' in order to break laws (for instance, to block the transport of atomic waste), the US government refers to a 'higher state of emergency' of saving humanity from the threats of nuclear, biological or chemical weapons terrorism in order to bypass the Security Council and to break the law of nations. Of course, the differences are striking: in the case of movements against the use of nuclear power, the idea of prevention encourages a discontinuation of nuclear power by peaceful means. On the other hand, in the case of the threat of terrorism the same idea of prevention provides a temptation to military invasions of foreign countries. Nevertheless, both anti-threat movements have one thing in common. In the eyes of Greenpeace, but also precisely in the eyes of the Bush administration, the prevention of a threat to humanity justifies the breaking of international and national law.

Who is going to liberate us from the visible enthusiasm in the eyes of those American world-redeemers? After all, the suspicion of terrorism gives the most powerful nation in the world the liberty to construct ever-shifting images of the enemy and the potential to defend their 'homeland security' everywhere with military force on the soil of foreign countries.

Although Americans and Europeans do not live, as Robert Kagan claims, on Mars and Venus, they nevertheless live in different worlds. As much as many Americans are absolutely certain about the 'reality' of a terrorism threat posed by ABC weapons, just as many Europeans are firmly convinced of other threats to humanity that seem 'hypothetical' and 'irrational' to many Americans: the threat of a climatic catastrophe, the genetically-altered 'Franken-Food,' and so on. The social-scientific study of threats teaches us that they are and become real because they exist in the eye of the beholder. The reality and the perception of danger are difficult to separate. To put it more clearly, in the end, there is no 'reality' of threats independent of cultural perception and assessment. The 'objectivity' of a threat exists and arises essentially from the belief in it.

This 'objectivity' must 'render' itself in global, public discourse, in regard to the threat both of nuclear power and of nuclear terror, and must be etched into the heads and hearts of people through global information and symbols. Whoever believes, however, in a specific threat lives in a different world from the person who does not share this belief and might consider it hysterical. The rift causing division within the Western alliance, which threatens to cause the failure of NATO and seems to fundamentally change the European Union, has its roots in the denial or rather the recognition of threats that some consider existential, others nonsensical, pathological, and hostile to science.

III

September 11 is, however, also the Chernobyl of the military concept of power. The equation 'arms build-up equals safety' is no longer valid. Threats and insecurities are not a distinct feature of Second Modernity; rather, people are confronted with them at all times and in all cultures. The specifically new thing that entered the world in and through the terrorist dimension of a world risk society is now precisely that even the most powerful nations, in the brilliance of their absolute military superiority, are almost defenseless against the attacks of anonymous, unpredictable, and uncontrollable sources of violence. As a result, two premises of the present Neorealistic theory of the state collapse: the strongest is no longer protected against attacks by the weakest. Indeed, statehood sees itself called into question because its classical means of defense against aggressions are no longer effective. Even the most highly sophisticated, the most perfect military power that world history has ever produced, faces terror attacks, to which the principle of deterrence or the idea of the external enemy no longer applies (the enemy is rather simultaneously both inside and outside of the attacked society), with almost pacifistic helplessness. This world power can militarily conquer even the most remote corners of the world, but it will not renew the control exercised by the state and will instead actually increase its vulnerability. The 'conquered' Iraq is already one example: the soldiers who, in their cultural ignorance, grope around in foreign cultures, become targets of terrorist attacks. This is, however, exactly what potentially changes everything: the institutionalized and perfected forms of military power of the highly sophisticated state *fail* in view of terrorist threats. It is no less than the modern archetype of the invulnerability of state power which was founded on military power – the more superior the military power, the more powerful and invulnerable the state – that is destroyed by the global dangers of a world risk society. People and cultures have always been seized by paranoid fears. That this can now also be said for the (mega)state power itself is the historical novelty in the epoch of a world risk society.

What possibility remains for states, regardless of their strength, to deal with these new dangers? In the end, there is only one thing to do. They must cut the new dangers in such a way that they will fit into the boxes of old terms and institutions. In this case, that means: America's fear of vulnerability must be combated with established means of military strength. This means that the war against anonymous terrorism must be fought as a war against evil and weak states. Kagan's diagnosis is therefore wrong; no insurmountable abyss has opened up in the relation between the United States and Europe, but a new, tacit commonality has developed. For entirely different reasons, both sides downplay the novelty of terrorist threats. The US does so because the 'war' against terrorism precisely cannot be a war against nations if it wishes to be effective and not counterproductive. Europe does so because, if it were to accept the novelty of terrorist threats, the insight into its vulnerability would result in the loss of the inner balance inherent in its politics of military abstinence.

IV

Neorealism and its military autism of power have another birth defect: they assume that violence creates justice and legitimacy and thus fail to see that, in a world risk society, the legitimate sources of violence have shifted from the national to the global context. On the one hand, the battle against threats to civilization becomes a foundation of *legitimate* global dominion. In other words, next to what Max Weber described as the legitimate sources of dominion, all of which are situated within the framework of the nation-state, in the age of global threats, a representative battle is fought against dominion as a means of legitimizing no longer only a national but a transnational exercise of power and dominion. Those who benefit from this development are advocacy groups, but also big companies that succeed in establishing ecological norms of production, condemn child labor and transnationalize labor rights; but also precisely those countries that get actively involved in the worldwide fight against terror networks and the opposition against violations of human rights and genocide.

On the other hand, the 'rule of law' in international relations also develops an innovative, global effectiveness. The example of the human rights regime can be used to show this. The power of humanitarian law to create rhetoric and legitimacy has grown exponentially, something that shows itself in its spatial and temporal expansion, in the changed understanding of individual civil rights and liberties, as well as in a new institutionalism. The human rights regime undermines the old territorial logic of nation-state law; it is no longer solely in effect in times of war, like the humanitarian law. On the contrary, it is now applied in general – which means also in times of peace and also beyond the borders of nation-states – to domestic conflicts within realms of state sovereignty. All this is expressed in new contracts, institutions, controls, and tribunals, including the International Court of Justice. In other words, the legitimacy of transnational military uses of power is not automatically the product of military strength, but rather depends on the adherence to newly emerging, global legal principles and procedures to which it is linked. To put it differently, in a world risk society, global political power is not the product of military strength (according to the equation: the greater the military superiority, the greater the political power); rather, what counts is that only that military power which voluntarily subjects itself to the dominion of the law in a global realm, and binds itself to it, can create political power.

Whoever does the opposite and attempts to apply their national perspective to global problems (terrorism, questions of disarmament, climatic catastrophe, etc.), as the US does in an exemplary manner, gets caught up in the risks inherent in global interdependence. The national approach against transnational terrorism – closing the borders, surveying harbors, tightening air security, introducing new forms of 'homeland security' (see 'container idea'!) – literally falls short, and represents much rather the 'phantom-reaction' of the national at a time in which the causalities of problems no longer obey the schematics of the national. However, if the causes of, for example, terrorism, which are situated outside the national realm, are likewise fought against with a national and now military strategy – which means that cosmopolitan answers by other states aimed at cooperation are rejected – then this is not a strategy of strength but a strategy of weakness. In other words, in a world risk society, military strength turns easily into a weakness because it does not solve problems but rather increases them.

Accordingly, the unleashed world power has brought a second world power into the arena: the general public. Even the pro-American European governments had to swear loyalty to the 'coalition of the willing' against the overwhelming majority of their populations. The absolute predominance of the US can rely upon its weapons, but not on opinions, convictions, and consensus. However, that means that it already exists only as a destructive, self-disintegrating force that causes resistance against the US to flourish even in US-friendly societies and governments. This resistance is further inflamed by the breach and anticipated collapse of that world legal system which the US founded, in the spirit of an early cosmopolitan realism, after the Second World War and which they are now threatening to destroy. The re-nationalization of the United States goes hand in hand with the non-adherence to the Kyoto Protocol on climate protection, the contempt for the International Criminal Court, and the refusal to acknowledge the worldwide biological-weapon convention. All these legal foundations serve a double purpose: they are supposed to reduce the self-created threats to civilization *and* guarantee a reciprocal system of balance between hegemonic 'perpetrators' and 'victims.'

V

Neorealism misjudges the *new modes of power* that are precisely not a product of military strength but of the art of cooperation and the specific use of new, non-military sources of legitimacy of global power. There are principally two sides to the dangers that threaten states: they abolish the borders between national and international, but at the same time also relativize the asymmetry of power relations. Even the most powerful nation in the world is impotent in light of this threat. Unilateral efforts are ineffective or counterproductive. In order to preserve and increase their power, states must (a) cooperate, and (b) negotiate international regulations and establish corresponding international institutions. In other words: because nations wish to survive, they will have to collaborate. However, lasting cooperation changes the very essence of their self-definition. Their egoism of survival and of expansion of power forces their fusion and self-transformation. To put it differently, not rivalry but cooperation maximizes national interests. There is a way of pursuing national interests that is self-destructive (national autism), and another that maximizes power (cosmopolitan realism).

A world risk society necessitates a complex understanding of state power in which the military component is still important, but no longer possesses an all-decisive, monopolistic significance. It is also not sufficient, as Joseph S. Nye suggests, to differentiate only between various dimensions of power – military power, economic power, social power, and transnational obligation as well as moral power – that is, between 'hard power' and 'soft power.' After all, by doing so, the particular interdependencies and reciprocal limitations, as well as the inner contradictions between these individual components, remain underexposed; in particular, the decisive question is not even raised: what are the foundations of the legitimacy and, consequently, the stabilizers of global power? What significance does the way in which we publicly deal with the threats to civilization or the globalized dominion of law have for the exercise of military power?

Kagan's formula of 'power and weakness' must, therefore, be looked at differently if the actual power relations between the US and Europe in a world risk society are to be understood. The world order is not so simple that power and weakness could be clearly ascribed – power to the US and weakness to Europe. A closer look reveals that both are strong and weak at the same time; although the US possesses the military capacities, it nevertheless lacks moral and legitimizing power; the Europeans are militarily weak but have the legitimizing power of morality and law. One will not be able to easily change this peculiar mirror-inverted constellation of power *and* weakness on this side as well as on the other side of the Atlantic. As unlikely as it is that Europe will militarily draw level with the US in the foreseeable future, it is just as unlikely – even more so after the political damage subsequently caused by the Iraq war – that the US will be able to compensate for its worldwide deficit in legitimate authority. This could be – and this is the punch line – the foundation for a new transatlantic division of labor, a new transatlantic project: the United States urgently needs allies that can help it erect a feasible international order. Conversely, for the foreseeable future, the United States offers for Europe the only realistic chance to realize a world order that deserves this designation.

The deficit in strategic thinking proves to be the actual Achilles' heel of Europe. There is no agenda that could help Europe orient itself in crises and conflict situations. This agenda is lacking in the transatlantic debates as well as in the Near East, for the ethnic exclusions in the Caucasus as well as in Southeast Asia, for the Kashmir conflict as well as for the disintegration of states in Africa. Only when Europe succeeds in developing a culture of world-political thinking will it assume a prominent and relevant role in the shaping of the world. In other words, what Europe needs most urgently is a rational calculation of its cosmopolitan interests. Europe must overcome its tendency to be self-absorbed, and finally turn into a cosmopolitan Europe.

Previously unpublished

ANTI-AMERICANISM IN EUROPE:

From Elite Disdain to Political Force

Andrei S. Markovits

One need not be a diligent student of survey research to know that antipathy towards America and Americans has become a worldwide phenomenon. Just a glance at newspaper headlines, editorials, and television talk-shows, as well as casual conversations at parties and dinner tables, reveal a widely held hostility towards the United States that is seemingly unprecedented. A steady – and growing – resentment of the US (indeed, of most things American) has permeated European discourse and opinion, in particular, since the fall of the Soviet Union in 1991 and the corresponding end of the bipolar Cold War order that had dominated Europe since 1945. However, this antipathy has a very long and fertile history.

Anti-Americanism is a particularly murky concept because it invariably merges antipathy toward what America *does* with what America *is*. It is like any other prejudice insofar as its holder 'pre-judges' the object and its activities apart from what transpires in reality. Where it differs from 'classical' prejudices such as anti-Semitism, homophobia, misogyny, and racism, however, is in the fact that, in contrast to these latter cases – where Jews, gays and lesbians, women, and ethnic minorities rarely, if ever, have any actual power over the majority of populations in most countries in which they reside – the real existing United States most certainly does have power, and plenty of it. In contrast to these other prejudices – which have by and large become publicly illegitimate in most advanced industrial democracies – anti-Americanism thus remains not only accept-able in many public circles, but even commendable, indeed, a badge of honor, and perhaps one of the most distinct icons of being a progressive these days. After all, by being anti-American, one adheres to a prejudice that *ipso facto* also opposes a truly powerful force in the world. Thus, in the case of anti-Americanism, one's prejudice partially assumes an antinomian purpose, thereby attaining a level of legitimacy in certain circles that other prejudices – thankfully – no longer enjoy.

For hundreds of years now, Europeans and Americans have created imagined versions of each other that have served all kinds of purposes, not least of which was to delineate a clear 'other' for themselves. These mirror images have been rightly characterized as a 'compulsive *folie à deux*.' Yet there is an impor-tant difference in the respective agencies of this *folie à deux* on the two continents. In the US the carriers of prejudice and antipathy toward Europe have predominated, if at all, in the lower social strata. In contrast, American elites – particularly cultural ones – have consistently extolled Europe, and continue to do so. This love for and emulation of European tastes, mores, fashions, and habits remained a staple of American elite culture even during the country's most nativist and isolationist periods. Virtually all of America's high-brow culture continues to be European in derivation. One need only look at the humanities departments of any leading American university to observe this continuing cultural hegemony, which remains European in orientation even as it attempts to negate its Eurocentrism. Any resentment of Europe by American mass opinion has been of a completely different order of magnitude than anti-Americanism's presence in Europe. 'Freedom fries' never had any traction, and 'Europe' as well as the adjective 'European' continue to conjure up quality, excellence, desirability, and 'class' in most venues of the American vernacular. Terms analogous to 'anti-Americanism' – such as 'anti-Europism' or 'anti-Europeanism' – do not exist. Americans in their history have been known to be anti-French, anti-German, anti-Russian, anti-British, anti-Communist but never anti-European. To be sure, one important aspect of acculturation to America was to oppose things from 'the old country,' to try to distance oneself from the 'old world' in an attempt to create a new one. In that sense, one could speak of a distancing from Europe. But this never attained the degree of aversion that anti-Americanism has had for Europeans. And here, too, there are huge differences by social class and status. 'Ordinary' Europeans have never – at least until now – exhibited the aversion towards America that has been held by their elites. Indeed, as demonstrated by regular public opinion surveys since the 1950s, a solid majority of Europeans have expressed positive views of America, with only about 30 percent holding negative ones. Tellingly, the higher one proceeds on the social scale of the respondents, the greater the extent of negative attitudes towards America becomes. As such, anti-Americanism is arguably one of the very few prejudices in contemporary Europe that correlate positively with education and social status: the higher the education, the greater the prejudice. To European elites, America has always represented the epitome of tastelessness, inauthenticity, mediocrity, vulgarity, venality – in short, an inferior entity. Yet, these elites also resented America as a threatening parvenu, and they did so well before the US possessed any power that rivaled those of the established European states. While European elites disdained America, they also found it profoundly threatening and unsettling, not least because it embodied such an eerie attraction to Europe's masses – certainly not the elites' friends – and willy-nilly represented modernity and the future. In sum, European masses have by and large liked and respected America while European elites have certainly not, whereas American elites have liked and respected Europe but American masses much less so.

Lest there be any misunderstanding about what exactly I mean by anti-Americanism, here is the definition offered by Paul Hollander in his definitive book on the subject: 'Anti-Americanism is a predisposition to hostility toward the United

States and American society, a relentless critical impulse toward American social, economic, and political institutions, traditions, and values; it entails an aversion to American culture in particular and its influence abroad, often also contempt for the American national character and dislike of American people, manners, behavior, dress; and a firm belief in the malignity of American influence and presence anywhere in the world.'[1]

Whereas there was still a clear disconnection between elite and mass opinion in Europe following the 9/11 tragedy – with the former venting its *Schadenfreude* barely 48 hours after the crime while the latter expressed genuine sympathy for the victims – there emerged barely two years later a hitherto unprecedented congruence of opinion among both segments of European society in the course of America's war with Iraq. What differentiates the current level and quality of European anti-Americanism from its earlier variants is the fact that, for the very first time in the history of European anti-Americanism, a solid majority of European publics also bear substantially negative attitudes towards the United States, and their views thus converge on this topic – perhaps for the first time – with those of their elites. In no other instance in Europe's postwar development has there been such a complete convergence of views between elites and masses, between government and opposition, and among voices on the left and the right, as occurred during the four months of build-up to the war with Iraq. Anti-Americanism certainly preceded the Bush administration's policies, but it was they that created a hitherto unprecedented congruence between elites and masses in terms of their common antipathy towards the US. While the thrust of this antagonism focused on America's actions, its palpable passion was deeply anchored in what Europeans perceived as America's very core, its identity. To many Europeans, even in the countries where the governing elites maintained the deeply unpopular position of supporting the United States in its imminent war with Iraq – Britain, Spain, and Italy come to mind – America had become the 'un-Europe,' a clear 'other.' This othering was, of course, not totally new and had many precedents. Even under the aegis of Bill Clinton, whom European intellectuals embraced wholeheartedly as a kindred spirit, Europeans commenced the conscious construction of Europe as America's other. 'Europe: The Un-America' proclaimed Michael Elliott in an article published in *Newsweek International* in 2000, in which he dismissed any semblance of a common transatlantic civilization. Many European intellectuals appropriated Samuel Huntington's controversial notion of the 'clash of civilizations' as a way of characterizing what they perceived as the increasing divergence between Europe and the US and not – as Huntington had it – a clash between the predominantly Christian West and the Islamic world. The widely voiced indictment accused the US of being retrograde on three levels: moral (America as the purveyor of the death penalty and of religious fundamentalism, as opposed to European abolition of the death penalty and adherence to an enlightened secularism); social (America as the bastion of what former German Chancellor Helmut Schmidt called 'predatory capitalism' and of mass incarceration, as opposed to Europe as the home of the considerate welfare state and of rehabilitation); and cultural (America the commodified vs. Europe the refined; America the prudish and prurient vs. Europe the savvy and wise).

It was well before George Bush was running for president that French foreign minister Hubert Védrine inveighed against the US as a 'hyperpower' – *hyperpuissance* – which needed to be brought down by an 'un-American' Europe, obviously led by France. For Védrine, the clarion call of Europe's challenge to the US centered on the following American-inspired ills: 'ultraliberal market economy, rejection of the state, non-republican individualism, unthinking strengthening of the universal and "indispensable" role of the USA, common law, Anglophonie, Protestant rather than Catholic concepts.'[2] The points raised by Védrine bespoke a veritable *Kulturkampf* between 'Europe the good and America the bad.' Indeed, the term *Kulturkampf* is often used as a rallying cry by German intellectuals and cultural elites in their battles against the United States. Thus, the well-known German director Peter Zadek has said, '*Kulturkampf*? Count me in. I deeply detest America.'[3] Overt hostilities in language and attitude that are taboo among European intellectuals and elites if invoked against any other culture or country have attained acceptability when the US is concerned. Take the comments of British novelist Margaret Drabble: 'My anti-Americanism has become almost uncontrollable.'[4]

To be sure, the Bush administration's demeanor and actions have contributed to intensifying and legitimating this *Kulturkampf* among European publics to a degree hitherto unimaginable. No mobilization around the European counter-values adumbrated by Védrine could have been more emphatic than the huge demonstrations on Saturday, February 15, 2003. Never before in Europe's history did so many millions of Europeans unite in public on one day for one purpose. From London to Rome, from Paris to Madrid, from Athens to Helsinki, from Berlin to Barcelona, Europeans across most of the political spectrum united in their opposition to the impending American attack of Iraq. A number of European intellectuals proclaimed this day as the one that historians will someday view as the true birthday of a united Europe, precisely because like no other day in European history it united Europeans emotionally, and not only by fiat of a faceless bureaucracy issued in impenetrable language from Brussels.

At least to my knowledge, the first and most emphatic interpretation of February 15, 2003 as Europe's nascent national holiday was offered by Dominique Strauss-Kahn in a lengthy article in *Le Monde*. Strauss-Kahn could not have been more explicit about the significance of the demonstrations: 'On Saturday, February 15, 2003, a nation was born on the streets. This nation is the European nation.' Strauss-Kahn makes it unmistakably clear that the only commonality of this nascent nation lies in its opposition to the United States. Lest there be any misunderstanding that this sense of commonality pertains only to policy interpretations, political rivalries, or differences in interest, he leaves no doubt that he sees the chasm between Europe and the US as a matter of something much deeper, much more irreconcilable – namely, one of values, identity, essences.

Scarcely two months later, Jürgen Habermas entered the fray with a hitherto unprecedentedly coordinated endeavor. On May 31, 2003, Habermas published an article in Germany's paper of record, the *Frankfurter Allgemeine Zeitung*, on Europe's rebirth following the war in Iraq. Co-authored with Jacques Derrida, a French version of the piece was also published in *Libération*. On the same day, Habermas's friend, the American intellectual Richard Rorty, published a supportive piece in the *Süddeutsche Zeitung*, Germany's other paper of record and the *FAZ*'s main rival. Meanwhile, Adolf Muschg wrote in the eminent Swiss paper *Neue Zürcher Zeitung*, Umberto Eco in *La Repubblica*, Gianni Vattimo in *La Stampa*, and Fernando Savater in *El País*. These other contributions were independent articles, connected to the Habermas–Derrida piece only by a common theme: The war in Iraq was to be the clarion call for a European nation which all writers (with the possible exception of Eco) construed in explicit opposition to the United States. These intellectuals connected with a mobilized popular anti-Americanism that not only created the largest demonstration in European history on February 15, but that had also already permitted Gerhard Schröder to win one of Germany's narrowest parliamentary elections in September 2002 by running an explicitly anti-American campaign in which he constantly inveighed against 'amerikanische Verhältnisse' (American conditions) and promised his receptive voters never to allow those to become reality in Germany. America as a negative entity had developed into a potent and legitimate mobilizing factor in European politics.

To be sure, the Habermas initiative conspicuously excluded intellectuals from Britain, the Scandinavian and Low Countries, and especially Eastern Europe. Indeed, even a cursory reading of the Habermas–Derrida text reveals how much its putatively 'European' vision consists largely of advocating a Franco–German core that is to lead Europe away from its tutelage to the United States. Habermas speaks openly about an 'avant-garde' (*avantgardistisches*) 'core Europe.' Apart from the text's dismissal of other options and its disregard for East Europeans and their five-decades-long experience under Communist rule, it is remarkable how German-centered the document is, particularly given its author's *bona fides* as a genuine *Weltbürger* (world-citizen). Tellingly, the only politician whom Habermas mentions by name is Germany's foreign minister Joschka Fischer. Moreover, Habermas centers his entire argument on the alleged hegemony of the following clearly preferable European values that he implicitly juxtaposes to their naturally inferior American counterparts: a large dosage of scepticism towards the market combined with an acceptance of the state as a major social actor; a cautious attitude towards technology; a secular conviction that rejects any kind of religiosity in public life. These alleged European virtues have been the staples of Europe's debate about America and Americanism at least since 1945, if not before. As we have already seen in the case of Hubert Védrine, many European intellectuals have listed them before.

But this was a particularly strange departure for Habermas. After all, more than any other postwar German intellectual, he had always argued that the greatest achievement of the old Bonn Republic was its unreserved acceptance of the West in all its forms: cultural, social, political. And it was obvious to anybody who listened at the time that, for Habermas, the West not only included but actually featured the United States. For Habermas, too, apparently, one aspect of 'othering' the US in the current European development is to claim a strong affinity with the 'genuine' United States that over the past decade or so seems to have lost its way. Thus, at least for liberals of Habermas's normative predilections, the new Europe is not only the 'un-America' but actually a sort of 'ur-America.'

At the end of the day, the debate about America and the various views of America held by Europeans has little to do with the 'actually existing America' itself and everything to do with Europe. It is far from certain in which direction the tendencies analyzed here will proceed, since it remains equally uncertain where, how, and perhaps even whether Europe will develop into a more coherent entity. But one thing remains quite significant: Nobody ever spoke of Europe's birth being the fall of the Berlin Wall or the dissolution of the Soviet Union and its Communist rule over the eastern half of the continent. None of those events generated nearly the popular enthusiasm that February 15, 2003 did; indeed, while Berliners danced in the streets in 1989–90, Londoners and Parisians fretted in their homes. And nobody in Europe's West thronged public places in support of the celebrations in Warsaw and Prague during that period. Whether Strauss-Kahn, Habermas, and others will prove correct in arguing that this day will come to be regarded as Europe's birthday remains to be seen. One thing is evident, however: the long tradition of a deep ambivalence toward and a constant preoccupation with America in Europe clearly set the intellectual stage for the powerful symbolic presence of this potentially fateful day. History teaches us that *any* entity – certainly in its developing stages – only attains consciousness and self-awareness by defining itself in opposition to another entity. Every nationalism arose in opposition to another. With the entity of 'Europe' now on the agenda, anti-Americanism may well serve as a useful coagulating function for the establishment of this new entity. While it remains unclear what exactly ties Swedes to Greeks or Spaniards to Finns – especially on the all-important levels of emotions and identity – they clearly do share one important centripetal trait: they are *not* Americans. And since *not* being an American has attained such a potent and tangible political momentum in Europe's recent past, this fact cannot but enhance the meaning of what it is to be a European. Anti-Americanism in Europe has for the first time become a tangible political force on the mass level beyond the elite antipathy and resentment that has been a staple of European culture since at least July 5, 1776.

Previously unpublished

---

[1] Paul Hollander, *Anti-Americanism: Critiques at Home and Abroad, 1965–1990* (Oxford, 1992).

[2] Hubert Védrine, *Face à l'hyperpuissance* (Paris: Fayard, 2003).

[3] Peter Zadek, 'Kulturkampf bin ich dabei,' interview in *Der Spiegel*, July 14, 2003.

[4] Margaret Drabble, 'I Loathe America, and What It Has Done to the Rest of the World,' *Daily Telegraph* (London), May 8, 2003.

LITERATURE IS FREEDOM:

Speech on the Occasion of the Award of the Peace
Prize of the German Booksellers' Association,
Frankfurt Book Fair, October 2003

Susan Sontag

President Johannes Rau, Minister of the Interior Otto
Schily, State Minister of Culture Christina Weiss, the Lord
Mayor of Frankfurt Petra Roth, Vice-President of the
Bundestag Antje Vollmer, your excellencies, other distin-
guished guests, honored colleagues, friends ... among them,
dear Ivan Nagel:

To speak in the Paulskirche, before this audience, to receive
the prize awarded in the last fifty-three years by the German
Book Trade to so many writers, thinkers, and exemplary public
figures whom I admire – to speak in this history-charged place
and on this occasion, is a humbling and inspiring experience.
I can only the more regret the deliberate absence of the
American ambassador, Mr Daniel Coats, whose immediate
refusal, in June, of the invitation from the Booksellers'
Association, when this year's Friedenspreis was announced, to
attend our gathering here today, shows he is more interested
in affirming the ideological stance and the rancorous reactive-
ness of the Bush administration than he is, by fulfilling a normal
diplomatic duty, in representing the interests and reputation of
his – and my – country.

Ambassador Coats has chosen not to be here, I assume,
because of criticisms I have voiced, in newspaper and television interviews and in brief magazine articles, of the new radical
bent of American foreign policy, as exemplified by the invasion and occupation of Iraq. He should be here, I think, because

a citizen of the country he represents in Germany has been honored with an important German prize.

An American ambassador has the duty to represent his country, all of it. I, of course, do not represent America, not even that substantial minority that does not support the imperial program of Mr Bush and his advisors. I like to think I do not represent anything but literature, a certain idea of literature, and conscience, a certain idea of conscience or duty. But, mindful of the citation for this prize from a major European country, which mentions my role as an 'intellectual ambassador' between the two continents (ambassador, needless to say, in the weakest, merely metaphorical sense), I cannot resist offering a few thoughts about the renowned gap between Europe and the United States, which my interests and enthusiasms purportedly bridge.

First, is it a gap – which continues to be bridged? Or is it not also a conflict? Irate, dismissive statements about Europe, certain European countries, are now the common coin of American political rhetoric; and here, at least in the rich countries on the western side of the continent, anti-American sentiments are more common, more audible, more intemperate than ever. What is this conflict? Does it have deep roots? I think it does.

There has always been a latent antagonism between Europe and America, one at least as complex and ambivalent as that between parent and child. America is a neo-European country and, until the last few decades, was largely populated by European peoples. And yet it is always the differences between Europe and America that have struck the most perceptive European observers: Alexis de Tocqueville – who visited the young nation in 1831 and returned to France to write *Democracy in America*; still, some hundred and seventy years later, the best book about my country – and D.H. Lawrence – who, eighty years ago, published the most interesting book ever written about American culture, his influential, exasperating *Studies in Classic American Literature* – both understood that America, the child of Europe, was becoming, or had become, the antithesis of Europe.

Rome and Athens. Mars and Venus. The authors of recent popular tracts promoting the idea of an inevitable clash of interests and values between Europe and America did not invent these antitheses. Foreigners brooded over them – and they provide the palette, the recurrent melody, in much of American literature throughout the nineteenth century, from James Fenimore Cooper and Ralph Waldo Emerson to Walt Whitman, Henry James, William Dean Howells, and Mark Twain. American innocence and European sophistication; American pragmatism and European intellectualizing; American energy and European world-weariness; American naiveté and European cynicism; American goodheartedness and European malice; American moralism and the European arts of compromise – you know the tunes.

You can choreograph them differently; indeed, they have been danced with every kind of evaluation or tilt for two tumultuous centuries. Europhiles can use the venerable antitheses to identify America with commerce-driven barbarism and Europe with high culture, while the Europhobes draw on a ready-made view in which America stands for idealism and openness and democracy and Europe a debilitating, snobbish refinement. Tocqueville and Lawrence observed something fiercer: not just a declaration of independence from Europe, and European values, but a steady undermining, an assassination of European values and European power. 'You can never have a new thing without breaking an old,' Lawrence wrote. 'Europe happened to be the old thing. America should be the new thing. The new thing is the death of the old.' America, Lawrence divined, was on a Europe-destroying mission, using democracy – particularly cultural democracy, democracy of manners – as an instrument. And when that task is accomplished, he went on, America might well turn from democracy to something else. (What that might be is, perhaps, emerging now.)

Bear with me if my references have been exclusively literary. After all, one function of literature – of important literature, of necessary literature – is to be prophetic. What we have here, writ large, is the perennial literary – or cultural – quarrel: between the ancients and the moderns.

The past is (or was) Europe, and America was founded on the idea of breaking with the past, which is viewed as encumbering, stultifying, and – in its forms of deference and precedence, its standards of what is superior and what is best – fundamentally undemocratic; or 'elitist,' the reigning current synonym. Those who speak for a triumphal America continue to intimate that American democracy implies repudiating Europe, and, yes, embracing a certain liberating, salutary barbarism. If, today, Europe is regarded by most Americans as more socialist than elitist, that still makes Europe, by American standards, a retrograde continent, obstinately attached to old standards: the welfare state. 'Make it new' is not only a slogan for culture; it describes an ever-advancing, world-encompassing economic machine.

However, if necessary, even the 'old' can be rebaptized as the 'new.'

It is not a coincidence that the strong-minded American Secretary of Defense tried to drive a wedge within Europe – distinguishing unforgettably between an 'old' Europe (bad) and a 'new' Europe (good). How did Germany, France, and Belgium come to be consigned to 'old' Europe, while Spain, Italy, Poland, Ukraine, The Netherlands, Hungary, the Czech Republic, and Bulgaria find themselves part of 'new' Europe? Answer: to support the United States in its present extensions of political and military power is, by definition, to pass into the more desirable category of the 'new.' Whoever is with us is 'new.'

All modern wars, even when their aims are the traditional ones, such as territorial aggrandizement or the acquisition of scarce resources, are cast as clashes of civilizations – culture wars – with each side claiming the high ground, and characterizing the other as barbaric. The enemy is invariably a threat to 'our way of life,' an infidel, a desecrator, a polluter, a defiler of higher or better values. The current war against the very real threat posed by militant Islamic fundamentalism is a particularly clear example. What is worth remarking is that a milder version of the same terms of disparagement underlie the antagonism between Europe and America. It should also be remembered that, historically, the most virulent anti-American rhetoric ever heard in Europe – consisting essentially in the charge that Americans are barbarians – came not from the so-called left but from the extreme right. Both Hitler and Franco repeatedly inveighed against an America (and a world Jewry) engaged in polluting European civilization with its base, business values.

Of course, much of European public opinion continues to admire American energy, the American version of 'the modern.' And, to be sure, there have always been American fellow-travelers of the European cultural ideals (one stands here before you) who find in the old arts of Europe correction and a liberation from the strenuous mercantilist biases of American culture. And there have always been the counterparts of such Americans on the European side: Europeans who are fascinated, enthralled, profoundly attracted to the United States, precisely because of its difference from Europe.

What the Americans see is almost the reverse of the Europhile cliché: they see themselves defending civilization. The barbarian hordes are no longer outside the gates. They are within, in every prosperous city, plotting havoc. The 'chocolate-producing' countries (France, Germany, Belgium) will have to stand aside, while a country with 'will' – and God on its side – pursues the battle against terrorism (now conflated with barbarism). According to Secretary of State Powell, it is ridiculous for old Europe (sometimes it seems only France is meant) to aspire to play a role in governing or administering the territories won by the coalition of the conqueror. It has neither the military resources nor the taste for violence nor the support of its cosseted, all-too-pacific populations. And the Americans

have it right. Europeans are not in an evangelical – or a bellicose – mood.

Indeed, sometimes I have to pinch myself to be sure I am
not dreaming: that what many people in my own country now
hold against Germany, which wreaked such horrors on the
world for nearly a century – the new 'German problem,' as it
were – is that Germans are repelled by war; that much of
German public opinion is now virtually pacifist!

Were America and Europe never partners, never friends? Of
course. But perhaps it is true that the periods of unity – of
common feeling – have been exceptions, rather than the rule.
One such time was from the Second World War through the
early Cold War, when Europeans were profoundly grateful for
America's intervention, succor, and support. Americans are
comfortable seeing themselves in the role of Europe's savior.
But then, America will expect the Europeans to be forever
grateful, which is not what Europeans are feeling right now.

From 'old' Europe's point of view, America seems bent on
squandering the admiration – and gratitude – felt by most
Europeans. The immense sympathy for the United States in
the aftermath of the attack on September 11, 2001 was genuine.
(I can testify to its resounding ardor and sincerity in Germany;
I was in Berlin at the time.) But what has followed is an
increasing estrangement on both sides.

The citizens of the richest and most powerful nation in
history have to know that America is loved, and envied ... and
resented. More than a few who travel abroad know that
Americans are regarded as crude, boorish, uncultivated by many
Europeans, and don't hesitate to match these expectations with
behavior that suggests the *ressentiment* of ex-colonials. And some
of the cultivated Europeans who seem most to enjoy visiting
or living in the United States attribute to it, condescendingly,
the liberating ambiance of a colony where one can throw off
the restrictions and high-culture burdens of 'back home.' I
recall being told by a German filmmaker, living at the time in

San Francisco, that he loved being in the States 'because you don't have any culture here.' For more than a few Europeans, including, it should be mentioned, D.H. Lawrence ('there the life comes up from the roots, crude but vital,' he wrote to a friend in 1915, when he was making plans to live in America), America was the great escape. And vice versa: Europe was the great escape for generations of Americans seeking 'culture.' Of course, I am speaking only of minorities here, minorities of the privileged.

So America now sees itself as the defender of civilization and Europe's savior, and wonders why Europeans don't get the point; and Europeans see America as a reckless warrior state – a description that the Americans return by seeing Europe as the enemy of America: only pretending, so runs rhetoric heard increasingly in the United States, to be pacifist, in order to contribute to the weakening of American power. France in particular is thought to be scheming to become America's equal, even its superior, in shaping world affairs – 'Operation America Must Fail' is the name invented by a columnist in the *New York Times* to describe the French drive toward dominance – instead of realizing that an American defeat in Iraq will (in the words of the same columnist) encourage 'radical Muslim groups – from Baghdad to the Muslim slums of Paris' to pursue their jihad against tolerance and democracy.

It is hard for people not to see the world in polarizing terms ('them' and 'us') and these terms have in the past strengthened the isolationist theme in American foreign policy as much as they now strengthen the imperialist theme. Americans have got used to thinking of the world in terms of enemies. Enemies are somewhere else, as the fighting is almost always 'over there,' with Islamic fundamentalism having replaced Russian and Chinese Communism as the implacable, furtive menace. And 'terrorist' is a more flexible word than 'communist.' It can unify a larger number of quite different struggles and interests. What this may mean is that the war will be endless – since there will always be some terrorism (as there will always be poverty and cancer); that is, there will always be asymmetrical conflicts in which the weaker side uses that form of violence, which usually targets civilians. American rhetoric, which doesn't necessarily coincide with public opinion, would support this unhappy prospect, for the struggle for righteousness never ends.

It is the genius of the United States, a profoundly conservative country in ways that Europeans find difficult to fathom, to have devised a form of conservative thinking that celebrates the new rather than the old. But this is also to say, that in the very ways in which the United States seems extremely conservative – for example, the extraordinary power of the consensus and the passivity and conformism of public opinion (as Tocqueville remarked in 1831) and the media – it is also radical, even revolutionary, in ways that Europeans find equally difficult to fathom.

Part of the puzzle, surely, lies in the disconnect between official rhetoric and lived realities. Americans are constantly extolling 'traditions'; litanies to family values are at the center of every politician's discourse. And yet the culture of America is extremely corrosive of family life, indeed of all traditions except those redefined as 'identities' that can be accepted as part of larger patterns of distinctiveness, cooperation, and openness to innovation.

Perhaps the most important source of the new (and not so new) American radicalism is what used to be viewed as a source of conservative values: namely, religion. Many commentators have noted that perhaps the biggest difference between the United States and most European countries (old as well as new according to current American distinction) is that in the United States religion still plays a central role in society and public language. But this is religion American style: more the idea of religion than religion itself.

True, when, during George Bush's run for president in 2000, a journalist was inspired to ask the candidate to name his 'favorite philosopher,' the well-received answer – one that would make a candidate for high office from any centrist party here in any European country a laughing stock – was 'Jesus Christ.' But, of course, Bush didn't mean, and was not understood to mean, that, if elected, his administration would actually feel bound by any of the precepts or social programs expounded by Jesus.

The United States is a generically religious society. That is, in the United States it's not important which religion you adhere to, as long as you have one. To have a ruling religion, even a theocracy, that would be just Christian (or a particular Christian denomination) would be impossible. Religion in America must be a matter of choice. This modern, relatively contentless idea of religion, constructed along the lines of consumerist choice, is the basis of American conformism, self-righteousness, and moralism (which Europeans often mistake, condescendingly, for Puritanism). Whatever historic faiths the different American religious entities purport to represent, they all preach something similar: reform of personal behavior, the value of success, community cooperativeness, tolerance of others' choices. (All virtues that further and smooth the functioning of consumer capitalism.) The very fact of being religious ensures respectability, promotes order, and gives the guarantee of virtuous intentions to the mission of the United States to lead the world.

What is being spread – whether it is called democracy, or freedom, or civilization – is part of a work in progress, as well as the essence of progress itself. Nowhere in the world does the Enlightenment dream of progress have such a fertile setting as it does in America.

Are we then really so separate? How odd that, at a moment when Europe and America have never been so similar culturally, there has never been such a great divide.

Still, for all the similarities in the daily lives of citizens in rich European countries and the daily lives of Americans, the gap between the European and the American experience is a genuine one, founded on important differences of history, of notions of the role of culture, of real and imagined memories.

The antagonism – for there is antagonism – is not to be resolved in the immediate future, for all the good will of many people on both sides of the Atlantic. And yet one can only deplore those who want to maximize those differences, when we do have so much in common.

The dominance of America is a fact. But America, as the present administration is starting to see, cannot do everything alone. The future of our world – the world we share – is syncretistic, impure. We are not shut off from each other. More and more, we leak into each other.

In the end, the model for whatever understanding – conciliation – we might reach lies in thinking more about that venerable opposition, 'old' and 'new.' The opposition between 'civilization' and 'barbarism' is essentially stipulatory; it is corrupting to think about and pontificate about – however much it may reflect certain undeniable realities. But the opposition of 'old' and 'new' is genuine, ineradicable, at the center of what we understand to be experience itself.

'Old' and 'new' are the perennial poles of all feeling and sense of orientation in the world. We cannot do without the old, because in what is old is invested all our past, our wisdom, our memories, our sadness, our sense of realism. We cannot do without faith in the new, because in what is new is invested all our energy, our capacity for optimism, our blind biological yearning, our ability to forget – the healing ability that makes reconciliation possible.

The inner life tends to mistrust the new. A strongly developed inner life will be particularly resistant to the new. We are told we must choose – the old or the new. In fact, we must choose both. What is a life if not a series of negotiations between the old and the new? It seems to me that one should always be seeking to talk oneself out of these stark oppositions.

Old versus new, nature versus culture – perhaps it is inevitable that the great myths of our cultural life be played out as geography, not only as history. Still, they are myths, clichés, stereotypes – no more; the realities are much more complex.

A good deal of my life has been devoted to trying to demystify ways of thinking that polarize and oppose. Translated into politics, this means favoring what is pluralistic and secular. Like some Americans and many Europeans, I would far prefer to live in a multilateral world – a world not dominated by any one country (including my own). I could express my support, in a century that already promises to be another century of extremes, of horrors, for a whole panoply of meliorist principles – in particular, for what Virginia Woolf calls 'the melancholy virtue of tolerance.'

Let me rather speak first of all as a writer, as a champion of the enterprise of literature, for therein lies the only authority I have.

The writer in me distrusts the good citizen, the 'intellectual ambassador,' the human rights activist – those roles which are mentioned in the citation for this prize, much as I am committed to them. The writer is more sceptical, more self-doubting, than the person who tries to do (and to support) the right thing.

One task of literature is to formulate questions and construct counter-statements to the reigning pieties. And even when art is not oppositional, the arts gravitate toward contrariness. Literature is dialogue; responsiveness. Literature might be described as the history of human responsiveness to what is alive and what is moribund as cultures evolve and interact with one another.

Writers can do something to combat these clichés of our separateness, our difference – for writers are makers, not just transmitters, of myths. Literature offers not only myths but counter-myths, just as life offers counter-experiences – experiences that confound what you thought you thought, or felt, or believed.

A writer, I think, is someone who pays attention to the world. That means trying to understand, take in, connect with, what wickedness human beings are capable of; and not be corrupted – made cynical, superficial – by this understanding.

Literature can tell us what the world is like.

Literature can give standards and pass on deep knowledge, incarnated in language, in narrative.

Literature can train, and exercise, our ability to weep for those who are not us or ours.

Who would we be if we could not sympathize with those who are not us or ours? Who would we be if we could not forget ourselves, at least some of the time? Who would we be if we could not learn? Forgive? Become something other than we are?

On the occasion of receiving this glorious prize, this glorious *German* prize, let me tell you something of my own trajectory.

I was born, a third-generation American of Polish and Lithuanian Jewish descent, two weeks before Hitler came to power. I grew up in the American provinces (Arizona and California), far from Germany, and yet my entire childhood was haunted by Germany, by the monstrousness of Germany, and by the German books and the German music I loved, which set my standard for what is exalted and intense.

Even before Bach and Mozart and Beethoven and Schubert and Brahms, there were a few German books. I am thinking of a teacher in an elementary school in a small town in southern Arizona, Mr Starkie, who had awed his pupils by telling us that he had fought with Pershing's army in Mexico against Pancho Villa: this grizzled veteran of an earlier American imperialist venture had, it seems, been touched – in translation – by the idealism of German literature, and, having taken in my particular hunger for books, loaned me his own copies of *The Sorrows of Young Werther* and *Immensee*.

Soon after, in my childhood orgy of reading, chance led me to other German books, including Kafka's 'In the Penal Colony,' where I discovered dread and injustice. And a few years later, when I was a high school student in Los Angeles, I found all of Europe in a German novel. No book has been more important in my life than *The Magic Mountain* – whose subject

is, precisely, the clash of ideals at the heart of European civilization. And so on, through a long life that has been steeped
in German high culture. Indeed, after the books and the music,
which were, given the cultural desert in which I lived, virtually clandestine experiences, came real experiences. For I am
also a late beneficiary of the German cultural diaspora, having
had the great good fortune of knowing well some of the incomparably brilliant Hitler refugees, those writers and artists and
musicians and scholars that America received in the 1930s and
who so enriched the country, particularly its universities. Let
me name two I was privileged to count as friends when I was
in my late teens and early twenties, Hans Gerth and Herbert
Marcuse; those with whom I studied at the University of
Chicago and at Harvard, Christian Mackauer and Leo Strauss
and Paul Tillich and Peter Heinrich von Blanckenhagen, and
in private seminars, Aron Gurwitsch and Nahum Glatzer; and
Hannah Arendt, whom I knew after I moved to New York in
my mid-twenties – so many models of the serious, whose
memory I would like to evoke here.

But I shall never forget that my engagement with German
culture, with German seriousness, all started with obscure,
eccentric Mr Starkie (I don't think I ever knew his first name),
who was my teacher when I was ten, and whom I never saw
afterward.

And that brings me to a story, with which I will conclude
– as seems fitting, since I am neither primarily a cultural ambassador nor a fervent critic of my own government (a task I
perform as a good American citizen). I am a story-teller.

So, back to ten-year-old me, who found some relief from
the tiresome duties of being a child by poring over Mr Starkie's
tattered volumes of Goethe and Storm. At the time I am
speaking of, 1943, I was aware that there was a prison camp
with thousands of German soldiers, Nazi soldiers as of course
I thought of them, in the northern part of the state, and,
knowing I was Jewish (if only nominally, my family having
been completely secular and assimilated for two generations,

nominally, I knew, was enough for Nazis), I was beset by a recurrent nightmare in which Nazi soldiers had escaped from the prison and had made their way downstate to the bungalow on the outskirts of the town where I lived with my mother and sister, and were about to kill me.

Flash forward to many years later, the 1970s, when my books started to be published by Hanser Verlag, and I came to know the distinguished Fritz Arnold (he had joined the firm in 1965), who was my editor at Hanser until his death in February 1999.

One of the first times we were together, Fritz said he wanted to tell me – presuming, I suppose, that this was a prerequisite to any friendship that might arise between us – what he had done during the war. I assured him that he did not owe me any such explanation; but, of course, I was touched by his bringing up the subject. I should add that Fritz Arnold was not the only German of his generation (he was born in 1916) who, soon after we met, insisted on telling me what he or she had done in Nazi times. And not all of the stories were as innocent as what I was to hear from Fritz.

Anyway, what Fritz told me was that he had been a university student of literature and art history, first in Munich, then in Cologne, when, at the start of the war, he was drafted into the Wehrmacht with the rank of corporal. His family was, of course, anything but pro-Nazi – his father was Karl Arnold, the legendary political cartoonist of *Simplicissimus* – but emigration seemed out of the question, and he accepted, with dread, the call to military service, hoping neither to kill anyone nor to be killed.

Fritz was one of the lucky ones. Lucky to have been stationed first in Rome (where he refused his superior officer's invitation to be commissioned a lieutenant), then in Tunis; lucky enough to have remained behind the lines and never once to have fired a weapon; and finally, lucky, if that is the right word, to have been taken prisoner by the Americans in 1943, to have been transported by ship across the Atlantic with other captured German soldiers to Norfolk, Virginia, and then taken by train across the continent to spend the rest of the war in a prison camp in … northern Arizona.

Then I had the pleasure of telling him, sighing with wonder, for I had already started to be very fond of this man – this was the beginning of a great friendship as well as an intense professional relationship – that while he was a prisoner of war in northern Arizona, I was in the southern part of the state, terrified of the Nazi soldiers who were there, *here*, and from whom there would be no escape.

And then Fritz told me that what got him through his nearly three years in the prison camp in Arizona was that he was allowed access to books: he had spent those years reading and rereading the English and American classics. And I told him that what saved me as a schoolchild in Arizona, waiting to grow up, waiting to escape into a larger reality, was reading books, books in translation as well as those written in English.

To have access to literature, world literature, was to escape the prison of national vanity, of philistinism, of compulsory provincialism, of inane schooling, of imperfect destinies and bad luck. Literature was the passport to enter a larger life; that is, the zone of freedom.

Literature was freedom. Especially in a time in which the values of reading and inwardness are so strenuously challenged, literature *is* freedom.

NOTES ON CONTRIBUTORS

Ulrich Beck, born 1944, is Professor of Sociology at the University of Munich and Visiting Centennial Professor at the London School of Economics and Political Science. He is editor of the journal *Soziale Welt* and of the series 'Second Modernity' for Suhrkamp, and is director of a German National Science Foundation (DFG) research center on 'Reflexive Modernization.'

Lord Ralf Dahrendorf was Director of the London School of Economics and Warden of St Antony's College, Oxford. He is a member of the House of Lords and the author of numerous publications on social and political subjects.

Jacques Derrida taught at the École Normale Supérieure and the Sorbonne. He was Director of Studies (Directeur d'études) at the École des Hautes Études en Sciences Sociales in Paris until his death in 2004.

Dan Diner is a Professor in the Department of History at the Hebrew University of Jerusalem and Director of the Simon Dubnow Institute for Jewish History and Culture at Leipzig University.

Umberto Eco is a novelist and writer whose works include *The Name of the Rose*, *Foucault's Pendulum*, and *The Island of the Day Before*. His most recent book in English is *Baudolino*.

Péter Esterházy, born 1950 in Budapest, studied mathematics at that city's ELTE University. He is author of several prose works – primarily novels, short stories, and essays – and of one drama. His works have been translated into more than twenty languages; *Celestial Harmonies*, *She Loves Me*, and *The Book of Hrabal* are available in English.

Timothy Garton Ash is the author, most recently, of *Free World: Why a Crisis of the West Reveals the Opportunity of Our Time*. He is Director of the European Studies Centre at St Antony's College, Oxford, and a Senior Fellow at the Hoover Institute, Stanford.

Mathias Greffrath is a sociologist who has been working as a journalist and author for major German papers, radio, and television. His current fields of interests are the social, psycho-logical, and political implications of globalization, molecular biology of emotions, and the history of enlightenment. He has published books on sociology, the anti-globalization movement, and Michel de Montaigne.

Dieter Grimm was a Justice at Germany's Federal Constitutional Court from 1987 to 1999. He currently teaches constitutional law at Humboldt University Berlin and at the Yale Law School, New Haven, Connecticut. He is Rector of the Institute for Advanced Study (*Wissenschaftskolleg*) in Berlin.

Jürgen Habermas is Professor Emeritus of Philosophy at the Johann Wolfgang von Goethe University in Frankfurt, and is currently Permanent Visiting Professor of Philosophy at Northwestern University. His most recent works in English include *The Future of Human Nature* (2003) and the forthcoming collection *Time of Transitions*.

Karl Otto Hondrich studied economics, politics, and soci-ology in Cologne, Berlin, Paris, and Berkeley. From 1963 to

1965 he taught at the University of Kabul, Afghanistan. Since 1972 he has been a Professor of Sociology in Frankfurt.

Harold James was a Fellow of Peterhouse, Cambridge, and is now Professor of History at Princeton University. His recent books include *The End of Globalization* (2001) and *Europe Reborn* (2003).

Jürgen Kaube, born 1962, studied Economics, Philosophy, and Art History at the Free University Berlin and was Assistant Professor of Sociology at the University of Bielefeld before he joined the Editorial Staff of the *Frankfurter Allgemeine Zeitung*, where he covers Higher Education, the Humanities, and Social Sciences.

Aldo Keel wrote his dissertation on the Icelandic writer Halldór Laxness. He has written biographies of the Norwegian writer Bjørnstjerne Bjørnson (Honnør-Prize of the Norwegian Freedom of Expression Foundation), the Danish writer Martin Anderson Nexø, and the German editor Albert Langen. He works as an editor, translator, and journalist.

Adam Krzeminski is publisher of the Polish magazine *Polityka*.

Gerd Langguth was born in 1946. He teaches Political Science at Bonn University.

Andrei S. Markovits is the Karl W. Deutsch Collegiate Professor of Comparative Politics and German Studies at the University of Michigan in Ann Arbor. His numerous writings on European politics have been published in nine languages. Markovits's current projects center on anti-Americanism and anti-Semitism in postwar Europe.

Adolf Muschg is Professor Emeritus of German at the Swiss Federal Institute of Technology, and a writer of novels, essays, and short stories. He was awarded the Büchner Prize in 1994 and is now President of the Academy of Arts in Berlin.

Ulrich K. Preuss is Professor of Law and Politics at the Free University Berlin and Judge at the Constitutional Court of the State (*Land*) of Bremen. His most recent book, *Krieg, Verbrechen, Blasphemie: Über den Wandel bewaffneter Gewalt* (2nd ed., 2003), deals with the legal and moral questions of the terrorist attacks of September 11 and the role of the US in international politics.

Gianni Riotta is a columnist for the Italian daily *Corriere della Sera*. His next book in English is *Alborada*, to be published by Harper Collins.

Richard Rorty teaches philosophy in the Comparative Literature Department at Stanford University.

Jan Ross, born in 1965 in Hamburg, is a staff writer for *Die Zeit*, the German weekly. His last book, published in 2000, was about Pope John Paul II.

Fernando Savater is Professor of Philosophy at Complutense University in Madrid.

Peter Schneider is a writer and lives in Berlin.

Gustav Seibt, a historian and literary critic, is author of *Rom oder Tod: Der Kampf um die italienische Hauptstadt* (2001). He is a member of the Deutsche Akademie für Sprache und Dichtung.

Susan Sontag is the author of four novels, including *The Volcano Lover* and *In America*; a collection of stories, several plays, and seven works of nonfiction, among them her most recent book, *Regarding the Pain of Others*. Her books are translated into thirty-two languages.

Barbara Spinelli is a columnist for the Italian daily *La Stampa*.

Joachim Starbatty was born in Düsseldorf in 1940. He has been Professor of Economics at the University of Tübingen since 1983, and is Chairman of the Aktionsgemeinschaft Soziale Marktwirtschaft.

Andrzej Stasiuk was born in Warsaw in 1960, and lives in the mountainous Besleid Nisti. A writer, poet, essayist, columnist, and critic, his twelve books have been translated into many languages.

Gianni Vattimo has been a professor of theoretical philosophy at Turin University – from which he also graduated in 1959 – for more than two decades. He is also a fellow of Italy's Academy of Sciences, vice-president of the Academia de Latinidade and a member of the board of several Italian and European journals.

Hans-Ulrich Wehler taught as a Professor of History at the University of Bielefeld and as a Visiting Professor at Harvard, Princeton, Stanford, and Yale. His latest publication is *A History of German Society, 1700–1949* (4 vols, 1987–2003).

Johannes Willms obtained his PhD in History at the University of Heidelberg. He has written several books on German and French history and is correspondent for cultural affairs for *Süddeutsche Zeitung*, based in Paris.

Iris Marion Young is Professor of Political Science at the University of Chicago. Her most recent book is *Inclusion and Democracy* (Oxford University Press, 2000).

INDEX